40 LETTERS TO WRITE

ANDREW FERGUS

HULTON EDUCATIONAL PUBLICATIONS

© *Andrew Fergus*
1972
ISBN 0 7175 05987

First Published 1972 *by*

HULTON EDUCATIONAL PUBLICATIONS LTD.,
RAANS ROAD AMERSHAM BUCKS HP6 6JJ

Reprinted 1974
Reprinted 1979

Reproduced, printed and bound in Great Britain by
Cox & Wyman Ltd., London, Fakenham and Reading

CONTENTS

1

SETTING OUT A LETTER

Every letter you write requires:
1. Your address.
2. The date.
3. The greeting (or salutation).
4. The ending (or complimentary closing).
5. Your signature.

These various parts are numbered in the letter below.

---

(1) 22, Sycamore Road,
 Dolworth,
 Lincs.

(2) 24th March, 1972.

(3)
Dear John,

   Thank you for your invitation. Jean and I would love to come over on Tuesday evening. We shall give you all our news then.

(4) Yours sincerely,

(5) Tom.

---

1. *Your Address*

   Notice the slope in the address. Each new line starts a little to the right of the line before.

   There is a comma after the road, a comma after the town and a full stop after the county.

   The comma after the street number is now optional.

2. *The Date*

The date starts directly under the street number.

Occasionally the all-figure form of the date is used, and in that case the slope is continued e.g.

> 14 Park Street,
> Maidstone,
> Kent.
> 4 — 5 — 72.

Unfortunately this can be dangerous. An American would read this date as April 5th, 1972, since the American practice is to put the month first in all-figure dates. Various Continental countries also have their own methods. In fact, the most common method is the year-month-day order. At the moment international agreement is being sought to standardise all-figure dates, but until such standardisation is achieved it is safer to write out the date in full.

3. *The Greeting*

There are several possibilities for starting any letter to a Mr John Smith—Dear John, Dear Mr Smith, or Dear Sir.

The rule is simple.

If you would normally call him John in the course of conversation, start the letter "Dear John". If you usually address him as Mr Smith, then that is the greeting to use in your letter.

Dear Sir (or Dear Madam) are forms reserved for business letters when you are writing to someone you do not know.

4. *The Ending*

There are three common endings used in letters—Yours sincerely, Yours faithfully and Yours truly.

"Yours sincerely" is the friendliest, "Yours faithfully" the most formal and "Yours truly" somewhere in between. A handy guide which is often used is "Yours sincerely" if you begin "Dear John", "Yours truly" if you begin "Dear Mr Smith" and "Yours faithfully" if you begin "Dear Sir".

8

5. *The Signature*

The rule here is that you write enough of the signature to let the person know from whom the letter comes.

In a business letter the full signature must always be used. In a friendly letter beginning "Dear John" only the Christian name would normally be necessary, but if there is any chance that you might be mistaken for anyone else, then the full signature should be used.

Notice that the signature starts a little further to the right than the ending, thus repeating the slope we had in the address. In a well laid-out letter the ending should also start exactly under the date and the street number, as shown by the dotted lines.

Exercise

Examine the following short letters. Each contains two deliberate mistakes. Point out the mistakes, then re-write the letters correctly.

292, Bell Street,
Kilmarnock,
Ayrshire.
24th March, 1972.

Dear Joe,

    I was thrilled by your news. I shall be in your area on Wednesday, when I hope to visit you and offer my congratulations personally.

Yours faithfully,
Edward.

136, Hill Street.
Maidstone,
Kent.

Dear Jean,

Thank you for your letter. I shall be over on Thursday week and we can discuss everything then.

Yours Sincerely,
Anne.

20, Hawthorn Place,
Elmwood,
Yorks.
3rd February, 1972.

Dear sir,

Would you please send me a copy of your catalogue for 1972.

Yours faithfully,
John.

2

THE FRIENDLY LETTER

Letters can be divided into two distinct groups—the friendly letter and the business letter.

The friendly letter, as its name implies, is a letter to a friend. The most common type is one which forms part of a regular correspondence between two people who live too far apart to see each other regularly. The letter becomes the lifeline of their friendship. It takes the place of conversation, giving all the news, gossip, etc., that friends would normally exchange daily.

It follows that this is the least formal of all letters. The general rule is to write as you would speak.

Certain liberties may be taken too with the form. Instead of beginning "Dear Jean", a mother writing to her daughter might begin "Dearest Jean", or simply "Dearest", or even "Darling".

The ending may be varied with such phrases as "Yours affectionately" or "Your loving mother".

It should be noted, however, that the rules of grammar and spelling are still as strict, and that a friend—just as much as a business acquaintance—deserves the courtesy of neat, legible handwriting.

Below is a typical friendly letter:

Dear James,

Thank you for your letter. It arrived yesterday just after I'd returned from having a tooth out at the dentist's and cheered me at a time when I was badly needing cheering.

I was so pleased to hear that you've been promoted I know what it means to you, and how hard you've worked for it. The extra money will no doubt prove useful, but I'm sure the real thrill was to realise that your efforts have been appreciated.

11

I was even more pleased with the rest of your news—that you hope to spend your summer holidays here. Of course, we'll put you up! The old lumber room has been redecorated and turned into a spare bedroom. It may not be quite luxurious enough for a newly promoted sales manager, but it has at least a bed and a wardrobe in it, and it will be wonderful to sit up half the night swopping reminiscences again.

Things have been fairly quiet here recently. About the only excitement was the tennis club dance last Saturday. All the usual crowd were there, and Bill Rogerson is back in town. Do you remember him—the one who joined the Merchant Navy? He is now studying for a navigation exam, and is on six months shore leave while he attends college.

Another meeting I had was with Old Mr Bennett, our chemistry teacher. He has retired now, and is very shortsighted. He insisted that he remembered me well, but he kept calling me Peter, so I suppose he must be confusing me with my brother.

Mother and father are both keeping well and send their regards. They are as delighted about the prospect of seeing you again as I am.

Do write and make the final arrangements—and, once again, heartiest congratulations!

Yours very sincerely,
Tom.

This is a good example of a well-written personal letter.

It is grammatical and well thought out. It starts—and this is essential—by answering the various points in the previous letter in the correspondence. Other points are taken one by one, and each new topic is given a new paragraph.

Although the letter is grammatical, it should be noted that there is nothing stilted about it. The writer writes more or less as he would speak. He is humorous, gossipy, friendly. It is, in short, a fine, relaxed, natural letter—and that is the whole secret of the type.

Exercises

Attempt any one of the following:

1. Imagine that you are James, and that you have just received the above letter from your friend, Tom. Write a suitable reply.

2. A friend with whom you occasionally correspond has written you a letter saying that the firm he works for has gone bankrupt, that he intends to emigrate to Australia, and that before he goes he hopes to marry a girl whom you both knew well in the past. Answer his letter, commenting on his news, and adding a little of your own.

3. You have just heard that your next door neighbour has had an accident during a ski-ing holiday in Austria and is now in hospital there. Write and commiserate with him in his misfortune, giving him all the news of what has been happening in the district since he left.

3

THE BUSINESS LETTER

A business letter may be defined as any letter intended to conduct business rather than promote friendship.

Its scope is therefore very wide.

It comprises all that vast business world of invoices, contracts, specifications, etc. It also includes all private letters written to achieve a specific purpose—everything from sending for a catalogue to applying for a job.

Style

The perfect business style can be summed up in three short sentences.

    (a) Be brief
    (b) Be clear
    (c) Be courteous.

(a) Brevity

A business letter—by definition—is written to a busy man. It will be only one of a considerable number of letters he receives that day. It follows that the chatty, gossipy approach of the friendly letter is completely inappropriate. As a general rule the best business letter is always the one which uses the least number of words.

(b) Clarity

As well as being brief, the letter must contain all relevant facts or details. These facts should be worked out carefully beforehand, then included in your letter in a short, logical sequence of paragraphs.

(c) Courtesy

All business letters should be courteous. They are written to achieve a specific purpose, and politeness is the surest way to achieve it.

In this connection it should be remembered that in your attempts to keep your letter brief you should carefully avoid making it so overbrief that it appears curt and impolite.

Lay-out

The lay-out of the business letter is the same as that for the friendly letter, with one notable exception. As well as your own address, the name and address of the person to whom you are writing must also be included in your letter.

This address appears immediately after your own address and the date, but it is placed on the left hand side of the page rather than on the right. It should also be noted that, unlike your own address, this address takes no slope.

A typical business letter would therefore look like this:

9, Barrington Crescent,
Torville,
Devon.
14th July, 1972.

The Manager,
Dido Ready Clean, Ltd.,
Park Street,
Torville.

Dear Sir,

Thank you for the leaflet outlining the services you offer.

Could you please arrange for a representative to call and discuss the cleaning of my dining room and sitting room carpets. The most convenient time would be any weekday between midday and four p.m.

Yours faithfully,
Edith Walker (Mrs.)

Exercises

Attempt one of the following:

1. Imagine you are the manager of the Dido Ready Clean firm and answer Mrs Walker's letter, making arrangements for one of your representatives to call.

2. Write to the manager of your local T.V. and radio shop, asking for a representative to call and demonstrate their latest colour television set.

3. Imagine that you have a child who has been under the doctor's care for a fortnight with bronchitis. He is returning to school today. Write a letter to his headmaster, explaining the reason for his absence, and requesting that he be excused swimming.

4

ADDRESSING THE ENVELOPE

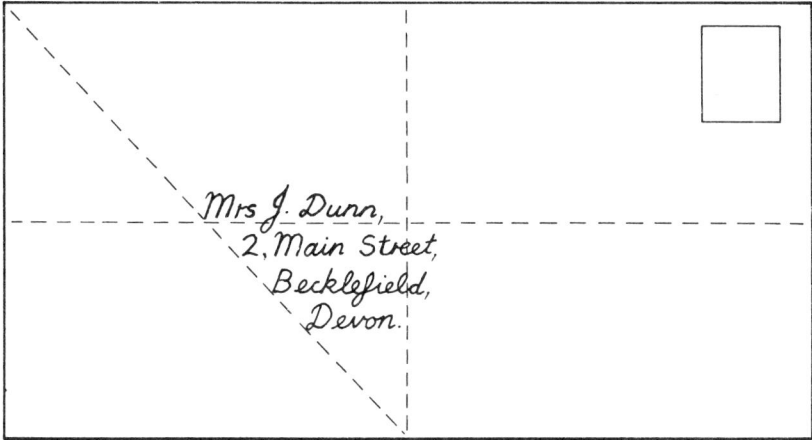

Above is an example of a correctly addressed envelope.

Notice the following points.

(a) The slope. Each new line starts a little to the right of the line before.

(b) The placing of the first line (the name) almost halfway down the page. The reason for this is that the stamp has to be franked, and if the name is placed too high it will be obliterated by the postmark.

Usual Forms of Address

A letter to John Smith should be addressed to John Smith, Esq., or J. Smith, Esq., or Mr. J. Smith.

Formerly the title of "Esquire" was reserved for people who owned land and "Mr." was the form of address reserved for someone in an inferior position. Nowadays, however, the distinction between the two has disappeared and "Mr." is considered equally correct.

If the person has a degree or distinction, "Mr" cannot be used. The form of address would then be John Smith, Esq., M.A. or John Smith, Esq., M.P.

A letter to a minister of religion should be addressed to "The Rev. John Smith", or, if a Catholic, to "The Rev. Fr. Gray".

A letter to a doctor should be addressed to John Smith, Esq., M.D., although modern practice now permits the less correct form, Dr John Smith.

All firms trading by name should have the word "Messrs" put before their name, e.g. Messrs A. R. Brown and Company, Ltd. Firms not trading by name do not take the "Messrs" e.g. The Atlas Mining Company, Ltd.

A woman is addressed as Miss J. Smith or Mrs J. Smith.

Two spinsters are addressed as The Misses Smith.

A boy under 14 is generally addressed as Master John Smith.

Officers in H. M. Forces are addressed by their rank and decorations, if any.

Here are a few addresses as examples:

(1)   J. Smith, Esq.,
                    7, Hawkhead Place,
                       Lindgrove,
                          Wilts.

(2)   The Rev. Robert Grant, B.D.,
                    The Vicarage,
                       Gransby,
                          Cornwall.

(3)   R. J. Smith, M.A., B.Sc.,
                    Managing Director,
                        Messrs Steed & Brown, Ltd.,
                        14, Main Street,
                         Cambuslang,
                            Lanarkshire.

(4)   Sq. Ldr. J. Brown, D.F.C.,
                           Officers' Quarters,
                           R.A.F. Leiston,
                           Saxmundham,
                           Suffolk.

(5)   Master J. Bradley,
                           Wilton House,
                           Easedale Preparatory School,
                           Limpington,
                           Warwickshire.

When a person is living temporarily at someone else's home, and there is any danger of confusion arising, the abbreviation c/o (care of) may be used.

(6)   J. Graham, Esq.,
                           c/o Jones,
                           114, Templeton Court,
                           London, S.W.2.

Counties

It should be noted that the abbreviated form of the county is often used. These are usually very obvious, such as Wilts for Wiltshire or Yorks for Yorkshire. Some, however, are not quite so obvious, and a list of these is given below.

Glos.	—	Gloucestershire
Hants.	—	Hampshire
Middx.	—	Middlesex
Mon.	—	Monmouthshire
Northants.	—	Northamptonshire
Oxon.	—	Oxfordshire
Salop.	—	Shropshire

Durham is usually written as Co. Durham.

Postcodes

These are a recent development. They were introduced as an aid to automatic sorting, and are now almost universal throughout Britain.

A postcode is a group of letters and figures which represent an address in abbreviated form. It should always be written in block letters and be the last item on the envelope.

The following are examples of postcodes:

> J. Brown, Esq.,
> 4, High Meadows Road,
> Purley,
> Surrey,
> C R 2   4 T J.

> The Secretary,
> National Savings Committee,
> 22, Melville Street,
> Edinburgh,
> E H 3   7 P E

Exercises

1. Draw an envelope, put in the guide lines, then address it to yourself. If you know it, include your post code.
2. Address envelopes to the following people:
   - *(a)* Agnes Brown, a spinster, who lives at 14, Grove Crescent in the Shropshire town of Holworth.
   - *(b)* Her father, John, who is a Member of Parliament.
   - *(c)* Her brother, Peter, who at the moment is at home, although he is a flight lieutenant in the Royal Air Force and has won the D.F.C.
   - *(d)* Her youngest brother, Robert, who is only 12 years old.

5

EXAMPLES OF VARIOUS BUSINESS LETTERS

In Chapter 3 it was mentioned that the scope of business letters was very wide. In this chapter an attempt will be made to give some idea of this scope.

We have already dealt with such simple business letters as a note explaining a child's absence from school and a request to a firm to send a representative to your home.

In this domestic sphere there are also such matters as writing for estimates, paying bills by post, demanding receipts, arranging appointments, employing tradesmen, complaining of bad workmanship or overcharging, requesting time to pay accounts, etc.

In the commercial sphere, apart from the various specialist functions which will be dealt with under separate headings, there are all the non-specialist letters like answering enquiries, sending out bills, acknowledging orders, issuing receipts, confirming details, etc.

The following are a representative selection of such letters. Note the style they are written in—crisp and concise, saying what they have to say logically and clearly, with not one word that is superfluous to their purpose.

Letter 1 *Paying a Bill*

The Manager,
Royal Garage,
Levington.

Dear Sir,
    Thank you for your letter of 14th August. containing your bill. I enclose a cheque for £14.50 to cover the amount.

Yours faithfully,
John Smith.

21

Letter 2 *Demanding a Receipt*

The Manager,
Royal Garage,
Levington.

Dear Sir,

On the 18th August I sent you a cheque for £14.50 to cover your bill for repairing my car.

As I reclaim some of this on my income tax return I require a receipt, and should be obliged if you could send me one at your earliest convenience.

Yours faithfully,
John Smith.

Letter 3 *Requesting a Repair*

Henry Lewis, Esq.,
House Agent,
49, Boscombe Street,
London, S.W.4.

Dear Sir,

The roof of the property I rent at 127 Main Street is leaking badly and causing dampness to spread through one bedroom.

I should appreciate it if you could arrange to have the damage repaired as soon as possible.

Yours faithfully,
Thomas Greene.

Letter 4 *Confirming an Appointment*

H. J. Hammond, Esq.,
Managing Director,
Ace Novelties, Ltd.,
4, Gresham Street,
Leeds.

Dear Sir,

Thank you for your letter of 12th June.

I shall be pleased to attend an interview at your office on 21st July at 10.30 a.m.

Yours faithfully,
Iain Symington.

Letter 5 *Answering an Enquiry*

L. Brown, Esq.,
Covington Yard,
Easingham,
Kent.

Dear Sir,

In reply to your enquiry of 14th August, we can supply 10 cm hinges in quantity at 28 p per pair, and can guarantee delivery within one week of receiving your order.

Yours faithfully,
Arthur Cowan.

Letter 6 *Acknowledging a Complaint*

J. Hardy, Esq.,
4, Hill Street,
Tormington,
Devon.

Dear Sir,

Thank you for your letter of 4th August.

Your complaint is receiving attention, and we hope to reply fully in a few days.

Yours faithfully,
Edward Finlay.

Letter 7 *Acknowledging an Order*

L. Brown, Esq.,
Covington Yard,
Easingham,
Kent.

Dear Sir,

I acknowledge receipt of your order for two thousand 10 cm hinges at 28 p per pair.

The order has been passed on to our despatch department and delivery should be made on the 4th or 5th of August.

Yours faithfully,
Arthur Cowan.

Letter 8 *Answering a Complaint re Non-Delivery*

L. Parsons, Esq.,
14, Seaview Terrace,
Redcar,
Yorks.

Dear Sir,
    In reply to your enquiry of 12th May concerning non- delivery,
your original order did not include your address.
    We have now sent off the materials you requested.

Yours faithfully,

Thomas Young.

Exercises
Attempt any two of the following:
1. Imagine that your teeth are giving you trouble. Write to
your dentist asking for an appointment.
2. You have received a complaint about non-delivery of an
order, but can find no trace of the order being placed. Write and
explain, asking for fuller details.
3. Three months ago you had two armchairs re-upholstered.
The fabric is now beginning to wear badly in several places. Write
to the upholsterer about it.
4. You work for a timber firm. A client has just written,
asking if you could supply a quantity of 1 cm thick whitewood
planks measuring 2 m by 60 cm. Reply to his letter.
5. You have just received a bill for £70. You wish to pay it in
two instalments of £35. Write, and request permission.
6. You bought a cigarette lighter at £2.50. Your neighbour
bought exactly the same lighter in another shop for £1.95.
Write to the manager of the shop about it.

6

THE THANK YOU LETTER

The first letter that most of us are called upon to write is the "thank you" letter.

It usually looks something like this.

Dear Uncle Peter,

Thank you for the lovely paintbox.

John.

When the paintbox becomes a cigarette case, however, and John himself becomes 18, something more is required.

That "something more" is precisely the difficulty with the letter of gratitude. Once you have said "thank you", what else can you write and yet still keep your letter firmly to the point?

A good example of how to overcome this difficulty is seen in the following letter by a twelve-year-old.

Dear Uncle George,

I was thrilled to waken on Christmas morning and find your present under the tree. I could scarcely believe my eyes. I know you promised me something extra-special for coming first in my exams, but never in my wildest dreams did I expect anything so generous.

It is a wonderful bike, especially the new five-speed gear, and it is the envy of all my friends. I have already been out on it, and as soon as the better weather arrives I intend to cycle over to Coniston to thank you in person.

Till then, please accept my thanks on paper.

Yours affectionately,
John.

Notice how the boy thanks his uncle, shares with him some of the excitement of when he first received the gift, expatiates on its good points, then links it very neatly with a promise of an early visit.

It is a short, natural letter, that carefully avoids the main pitfall of all such letters—the danger that it might degenerate into a long string of meaningless thank-you's.

Another thank-you letter which is very common is the letter of thanks for hospitality.

It is always polite to write a letter of appreciation for any hospitality which you receive, but if that hospitality includes an overnight stay then the letter of thanks becomes obligatory.

This is the well-known "Bread-and-Butter" letter. Only a short note is required, but once again the same difficulty arises—just what else to say once you have said "thank you".

A good example appears below.

Dear Mrs Grant,

I just had to write and thank you for the lovely weekend you gave me.

It was most kind of you to invite me, not only to Jim's party, but to stay overnight and come to Sunday's picnic as well. I enjoyed every minute of it, but I would like to make a special mention of that wonderful supper you served on Saturday night.

I only hope the extra work hasn't tired you, and would like to assure you once again how much it was all appreciated.

Yours sincerely,
Eric.

At first sight this letter might seem to break the general rule that Mr (or Mrs) takes the ending "Yours truly". This, however, refers mostly to business letters. With Mrs Grant the writer has a much more personal relationship and the "Yours sincerely" gives a warmer note to his letter.

Besides the more formal occasions which demand a letter of thanks there are, of course, innumerable other occasions when such a letter is required.

Take, for example, the case when someone has done you a service, such as keeping your pet while you go on holiday. A suitable letter of thanks would look something like this.

Dear Mrs Coulston,

Thank you very much for looking after Chico so well while we were on holiday. You have no idea what a comfort it was to know that he was with someone who loved dogs, and that he would be receiving at least as much care as we ourselves could have given him.

Now that he is back he shows not the slightest sign that he has missed us. Indeed when I had him out for his first walk last night he kept pulling me in the general direction of your house.

He really is in the most excellent condition. Thank you once again for all your kindness.

Yours sincerely,
Helen Webster.

Exercises

Write one of the following:

(a) A thank-you letter for an unexpected birthday gift.

(b) A Bread-and-Butter letter to an elderly aunt who has taken a cottage at the seaside for her holidays, where she has just entertained you for one very happy week-end.

(c) A suitable letter of thanks to a total stranger, who has found the library book you accidentally left on a train and has posted it on to your local library.

(d) You are the secretary of a club which is trying to raise funds in order to build new premises. A well-known local resident has just donated a handsome cheque. Write and thank him on behalf of the club.

7

THE MORE AMBITIOUS FRIENDLY LETTER— DESCRIPTION

The friendly letter has been defined as "conversation in writing."

That doesn't mean it must be mundane and commonplace. Just as good conversation can be an art, so too can good letter-writing. Examine the letter below.

Alpenhorn Hotel,
Gerstenhof,
Switzerland.
12th May, 1971.

Dear Helen,

Here I am at last in Switzerland.

The hotel nestles on a little ledge overlooking a lake as smooth and unruffled as any mirror.

From my window I look out on a fairy-tale castle—all towers and turrets. Beyond that the Alps stretch as far as the eye can see, range piled upon range, still covered in their winter snow.

As I am writing, a peasant woman is driving home the cattle, each one with a bell—yes, I swear it, a bell—around its neck.

The village is so quaint with its painted houses and carved woodwork that you almost expect Hansel and Gretel to emerge hand-in-hand at any moment from the forest.

Oh, how I wish you could have joined us here! Do write and tell me how you enjoyed Holland.

Yours from Wonderland,
Alice.

The writer has had an experience which she wishes to share with her friend.

She has sketched in the main features of the scene with a few imaginative strokes. To create atmosphere she has also chosen a unifying theme — the fairy-tale aspect — which she first introduces with the castle, carries through with the cowbells and the mention of Hansel and Gretel, and brings to a successful conclusion with a play on her own name.

Now try to write a similar descriptive letter on one of the following themes:—

1. Imagine you are Helen and reply in the same strain describing the scene from your hotel window in Holland.

2. You have been sleeping alone in the house and are suddenly jolted awake by a strange noise. Write a letter to a friend building up the feeling of tension and terror, then in the last line reveal the simple truth.

3. You have just returned from an opera, orchestral concert or beat group. You have still the feeling of excitement upon you. Write to a friend who has similar tastes trying to recapture for him in words the experience you have just enjoyed.

4. Imagine you have gone abroad for the first time. Nothing has come up to expectation. Your hotel is a hovel. All around are scenes of indescribable squalor. The sea is a distant smudge on the horizon. Paint a pen picture in a letter to a friend.

5. You are on a Mediterranean cruise and are standing on deck at night. On one side is Italy, on the other Stromboli is erupting, ahead lies tomorrow's port, and below is all the luxury of a first-class liner. Write a letter to a friend trying to capture the atmosphere.

8

FAULTS TO AVOID

In Chapter 3 the three main qualities of business letters were given as
- *(a)* Brevity
- *(b)* Clarity
- *(c)* Courtesy.

It should be remembered a good letter must satisfy all three conditions.

Take brevity, for instance. A man is sitting down to write a letter to his employers, asking for a rise. He is unsure what to write, then he remembers the motto — be brief.

He finishes up with a letter like this:

Dear Sir,

Can I have a rise?

Yours faithfully,
Robert Temple.

His boss, using the same admirable brevity, replies:

Dear Temple,

The answer is "No!"

Yours faithfully,
A. Nixon.

It is obvious that, though these letters may have brevity and clarity, they fall down completely on the third criterion. They are so short as to be positively discourteous.

Robert Temple should have given at least some reason for

asking for the rise. Mr Nixon should at least have made some excuse for not granting it.

The correspondence would then have read:

Dear Sir,

When I first joined the company in 1970 I was promised that my salary would be reviewed after a probationary period.

Since I have now been here for more than a year, may I suggest that an increase might now be considered.

Yours faithfully,
Robert Temple.

Dear Mr Temple,

Your request for an increase in salary has been put before the Board, but I regret that, owing to the present financial climate, they have found it impossible to grant.

Should you care, however, to re-apply in a few months, the matter will be given their sympathetic consideration.

Yours faithfully,
A. Nixon.

It should be noted in this respect that in an attempt to be over-courteous many writers seriously damage the clarity of their letters. Their letters become so flowery and longwinded as to be practically incomprehensible.

Examine the following letter:

Dear Sir,

I beg leave to thank you for your extremely kind communication in which you counselled me on the advisability of availing myself of your good services at as early a date as possible to obviate the disappointment of perhaps discovering that your exceptionally popular holiday cruises were unfortunately fully booked.

Much though I should be delighted to avail myself of your excellent advice, unfortunately my employers are not as considerate as your good self, and my vacation dates having not as yet been finalised completely, I must regretfully decline your thoughtful offer.

Yours faithfully,
Robert Gibson.

All the writer is trying to convey by this unspeakable drivel is:

Dear Sir,

Thank you for your letter advising me to book early.

Unfortunately, since my holiday dates have not yet been fixed, I find this impossible.

Yours faithfully,
Robert Gibson.

Exercises

A dealer has written, offering to sell you a second-hand car which you admired. You are interested, but do not want to buy it at the moment. You will not be using a car until the summer, so you do not want one before that and have all the expense of taxing it and insuring it. Write three letters:

(a) One too brief to be courteous.
(b) One too longwinded and flowery to be clear.
(c) One which you consider perfect.

9

THE LETTER OF CONGRATULATIONS

There are many occasions in life when congratulations are in order—an engagement, the birth of a child, a promotion, the successful passing of an important examination. At such times etiquette demands a brief letter from friends, and this presents certain difficulties.

Something just a little more enthusiastic is needed than "I congratulate you on passing your examination.

Yours sincerely,
Henry "

At the same time it is all too easy to become overfulsome and treat a promotion from Clerk Grade 2 to Clerk Grade 1 as if it were the presidency of the United States of America.

Steering a course between the two extremes is the whole secret of the good letter of congratulations.

Let us look at two actual examples.

Letter 1

Dear John,

I think it is absolutely marvellous that you have passed your final examination. I'm sure I don't know where you get all the brains.

It was so thrilling to see your name in print in today's Courier. It really is a wonderful achievement.

Medicine is such a worthwhile profession. I am always overcome with admiration for those who dedicate their lives to healing the sick.

Do call in and see us soon. We are all dying to inspect the new genius in the family.

I am so proud of my brilliant nephew. Many congratulations once again on your magnificent effort.

Yours sincerely,
Aunt Jean.

Letter 2

Dear John,

I was delighted to read in this morning's *Courier* that you had passed your final examinations, and I am sending this off right away in the hope that I may be one of the first to congratulate you.

I remember well how set you were on being a doctor, even as a small boy, and now that you have finally qualified the long years of study must seem very worthwhile.

Do call in and see me soon. I certainly don't want to lose touch with my favourite nephew—especially now that he is going to keep me healthy well into my nineties.

Yours sincerely,
Aunt Jean.

The first letter is one long gush.

It is full of the stereotyped phrases that bedevil so many congratulatory letters—"absolutely marvellous", "wonderful achievement", "worthwhile profession", "magnificent effort".

If it is examined carefully, it will become evident that the writer says nothing of any real moment after the first paragraph. The rest of the letter is taken up with repeating, in slightly different form, the original theme—the writer's breathless admiration for her nephew's brilliance.

The second letter, on the other hand, displays all the qualifications of the good letter of congratulations.

It is, first of all, completely natural. The writer manages to convey her enthusiasm without recourse to any stilted formal phrases.

Nor does she repeat herself. The second paragraph brings in two new aspects of the achievement—the long-standing nature of the ambition and the fact that it was not achieved without hard work.

Finally, in the last paragraph, she manages to lighten the tone of the whole letter with a jocular reference—still very much to the point—on her nephew's new profession.

Letters to Write

Choose any one of the following:

(a) A friend with whom you were at school has just become engaged. Write a letter of congratulations.

(b) A relative has just come first in his final law examination. Write and congratulate him.

(c) You have heard that an old friend has been promoted. Many years ago you remember him confiding to you that the post he has now been given was his greatest ambition. Congratulate him suitably on the promotion.

(d) You have been to a concert of either classical or popular music. One musician's performance has so moved you that you feel you must write and congratulate him. Do so, detailing the features of his performance which gave you so much pleasure.

(e) In this morning's paper you have just read about the birth of a son to the couple you met on holiday last year. Write a short congratulatory letter.

10

APPLICATION FOR A JOB

One of the most important business letters the average person is ever called upon to write is the application for a job. The care that should be taken with such a letter cannot be overstated.

When a firm advertises a job as vacant, then, if it is worth having, they may expect anything up to fifty or so applications for it. To interview such a number would be completely impracticable. The normal practice is to weed through the applications until they have a short list of three or four applicants, whom they call up for interview.

Your initial letter is therefore your only ambassador. On it alone you are judged.

With this in mind, it is surprising how little care some people take in the composing of a letter of application.

Neat and legible handwriting may not seem very important to you, but it almost certainly will to a prospective employer. A few blots and changes may not seem the end of the world, but they could mean the difference between your letter and the immaculate letter next to it on the pile being selected for the short list.

Apart altogether from the setting out of the letter, there are its contents.

Keeping in mind those fifty or so applications which the employer has to read, your letter should be kept as brief as possible, but at the same time you must give all the details which are relevant, and which will help a prospective employer to judge your suitability for the post.

What these details are will vary from post to post. For a salesman, for example, one of the most important facts might be whether or not he is in possession of a current driving licence.

There are, however, certain broad lines which can be laid down.

An applicant's age is always important.

So too is his education, especially if he is a younger candidate.

Any relevant experience which he has had should be included. It should be remembered in this respect that the experience need not necessarily have been gained at work. It could be some hobby or part-time pursuit that has a certain relevance to the post advertised.

There is also the very important question of the person's character. This can be gauged in one of two ways.

He may supply references. These are formal letters, written by people who know him well, testifying to his character and abilities.

It is important if such testimonials or references are being supplied that only copies should be sent. They are valuable documents, which you may need again, and it is all too easy for them to go astray. The applicant should, of course, be ready to produce the originals if called upon to do so at the interview.

Much more common today, however, is the naming of referees rather than the production of actual testimonials. All this involves is including in your application the names of people who know you well, and would be willing to supply references if called upon to do so This leaves the employer free to 'phone or write and put whatever questions he desires.

The normal number of referees required is two, and needless to say it is imperative that you obtain their permission before using their names.

Needless to say too there are certain referees who are more valuable than others.

No doubt your father or your Uncle Harry could be relied on to give you a glowing reference, but their word would hardly carry as much weight as that of a former employer. Other people who make acceptable referees include schoolmasters, ministers of religion, justices of the peace, and leaders of various leisure time organisations, such as youth clubs or further education centres.

These then are the main points which should appear in an

application for a job, and may be summarised thus:

(a) Age
(b) Education
(c) Experience
(d) References or Referees

It is also customary to state where you learned that the post was vacant, and some people include other details, such as the salary they expect, but unless such details are asked for specifically in the advertisement it is usually safer to omit them.

Following these instructions, then, a model application might look something like this:

9, Barton Street,
Greenton,
Lincs.
21st December, 1972

Personnel Officer,
Longwell Estates,
Greenton,
Lincs.

Dear Sir,

I wish to apply for the post of junior clerk advertised in the current issue of the "Free Press and Advertiser".

I am seventeen years of age, and, until last summer, was a pupil at Garbraid High School. There I took my "O" levels in English, History, Mathematics, French, and Commercial Subjects. Since then I have supplemented these qualifications by attending evening classes in the Pilton Commercial College, where I took Grade 1 passes in R.S.A. examinations in Typing, Shorthand and Book-keeping.

Since leaving school I have been employed as a junior clerk with the Linton Tool Company, but, since their office is small, I should prefer a slightly wider experience.

My personnel manager, Mr John Stewart, Linton Tool Company, Linton, and my former headmaster, James Edgar, Esq., M.A., 4, Longton Crescent, Linton, have kindly consented to act as referees.

Yours faithfully,
Margaret Brown.

Exercises

Apply for one of the following posts, inventing, where necessary, the appropriate qualifications and experience.

(a) Clerk Bookkeeper. Male or female. Must have experience of general office routine. Knowledge of stock control an advantage, but not essential. Apply to the Secretary, Bondmaster, Ltd., Malvern Industrial Estate, Malvern.

(b) Police Cadets. A number of vacancies are available now. If you are not less than 1 m 70 cm in height, between 16 and 18 years, athletically built, and have at least three "O" levels, apply to: The Chief Constable, County Police Headquarters, Blankshire.

(c) Shorthand Typist for duties in Accounts Department. This would suit an established junior looking for betterment. Ideal age would be a person over 18 years able to work on own initiative. Canteen facilities. Five day week. Applications in writing to Personnel Officer, Vanhill Concrete Company, Ltd., Bedford.

(d) A progressive company operating in the licensed and catering field wish to appoint managers capable of organising and controlling the catering side of their establishments. Applications, giving details of age and any experience, etc., are invited from those who have the ability and energy to participate where necessary in every aspect of the catering trade. An attractive salary will be paid. Current driving licence essential. Write to General Manager, Supafood, Ltd., Broad Street, London, W.C.2.

(e) Lasma General Insurance Company wish to recruit young school leaver who is interested in insurance as a career. Minimum educational standard, five "O" levels. Applications to Branch Manager, 12, Meadow Road, Hynes, Dorset.

(f) New venture. Activity Holiday Centre. Ski-ing, Boating, Climbing, Orienteering, Potholing. Bright young enthusiasts required as full-time wardens. Write, in the first instance, to J. Lawrence, Hillhouse Farm, Lawmuir, Selkirkshire.

11

THE MORE AMBITIOUS FRIENDLY LETTER—
HUMOUR

Of all the qualities a friendly letter can possess, none is more valuable than humour.

The occasional shaft of wit will brighten even the most mundane letter, but humour can do much more than that. On many occasions it can be used to take the sting out of an awkward situation.

Take the case of a friend who has stopped writing. You know his nature. He is a notoriously bad correspondent, and you are quite sure the long silence is due to his usual mixture of carelessness and laziness.

You could try to rectify the situation with the following letter:

Dear George,

It is now almost six months since I received your last letter. In that period I have written two, which have been left unanswered.

It really is a bit thick ! I have always been a very faithful correspondent, and I feel this is a poor return for my loyalty.

I am left in complete ignorance of all that is happening to you. I do not even know if you received the photograph I sent you in my last letter.

The only news I have had of you recently has come through your Uncle George, whom I meet occasionally. He assures me you are well, but beyond that I know nothing.

My own news I shall keep until I hear from you. Do write— even if it is only a short note.

Yours sincerely,
Arthur.

The most that can be said for this letter is that it is to the point. If George didn't feel like writing before, one can hardly imagine that he'll feel any more pleasantly disposed after receiving this long wail, full of injured innocence and holier-than-thou indignation.

Now let us see what humour can do. Let Arthur try the "mock terror" approach and send an alarmed, tongue-in-cheek little appeal:

Dear George,

Could you please kill some of the wild rumours circulating here.

Is it true that you have been taken over by Moon men? Have the Russians landed and transported you all to Siberia as slaves? Can plague really have wiped out everyone?

Just what, in short, is happening up there in darkest Lancashire? Are you alive or dead? Bankrupt or solvent? Drunk or sober?

It's now six months since your last letter, so — please! please! — if you still have the strength to lift a pen and the money to buy a stamp, do write and put your demented friends out of their misery.

Yours in the process of kitting out an expedition to come and search for you,

Arthur.

This letter makes its point at least as effectively as the last letter, but the humour robs it of all offence. The guesses at the reason for the silence are so wild, the mock alarm is so exaggerated that George can only laugh, then sit down and reply.

Another useful techniques is the "mock ignorance" approach.

Take the case of someone who has been advised by a Scottish friend to take his holidays in the Scottish Highlands. Having arrived there, he might send him a letter as follows:

44

Dear Duncan,

Here I am at last in the Highlands.

We were wakened this morning by a piper, and at lunchtime I had haggis. I've also tried speaking to quite a few of the locals, but I find the accent a little difficult.

On Saturday the Highland Games are to be held here, and several of the athletes are staying at my hotel. It is interesting to watch them practising, especially the caber tossers.

I am also most impressed by the scenery. Do try to come up here for a few days. I would love to see you.

Yours sincerely,
Roger.

Now notice how he brightens his letter if he adds a little humour and tries the "mock ignorance" approach, deliberately misunderstanding a few local customs.

Dear Duncan,

Here I am at last in the Highlands, and I'll say one thing for them—they're never dull!

I was awakened this morning by a terrible shrieking right under my bedroom window. Looking out in the half-light I saw a Highlander struggling with what appeared to be a tartan octopus on the lawn—and by the sounds coming from the octopus the Highlander seemed to be winning!

The food too is very adventurous. We had haggis at dinner. I might even have enjoyed it too if a perfect mine of information of a waiter hadn't insisted on informing me that it was made from various animals' entrails stitched up in a sheep's stomach.

Mind you, the natives are friendly. The first one I met greeted me warmly with what sounded very like "Hooroothenoo". I had just decided, to my horror, that he was speaking Gaelic, when I learned, to my even greater horror, that it was meant to be English.

However the scenery makes up for a lot. As I look out from my window at the moment everything is quietness and peace — except, of course, for some idiot in a tartan skirt who keeps tossing tree-trunks all over the lawn.

Do try to come up here for a few days. I'd love to see you — and I badly need an interpreter.

Hooroothenoo,

Roger.

Exercises

Write one of the following letters:

(a) A son has gone on holiday on his own. Always in the past after the first few days he has written home asking for more money. This time more than a week has gone past and the son has not yet asked for more. Write a letter to him, using the "mock terror" approach, suggesting some of the things that may have happened to prevent him asking for money.

(b) Choose any other country but Scotland and write a letter, using the "mock ignorance" technique, describing your holiday there.

(c) Write a letter to a friend, describing as amusingly as possible some event which has happened during your holidays.

12

THE INFORMAL INVITATION

One of the pleasantest letters to write is the informal little note inviting a friend round to your house. It would also appear to be one of the simplest, but appearances can be deceptive.

In actual fact the informal invitation is full of pitfalls. Examine the letter below:

17, Dunn Street,
Milton.

Dear Harry,

Just a short note to invite you round to our new house on Tuesday week.

We are all looking forward to seeing you very much. Helen sends her love.

Hope you can manage.

Yours sincerely,
Bill.

This may look a fairly typical informal invitation, but actually it is full of mistakes.

Let us list them:

1. The letter is undated.

2. The day of the visit is far too vague. Was the letter written before Tuesday? Does that mean the invitation is for next Tuesday or the Tuesday after that?

3. There has been no time suggested as to when the guest should arrive. Should he turn up at 6 o'clock and risk finding his host shaving—or leave it till 8.30 and risk having them all waiting for him hungrily so that they can start dinner?

47

4. Is there even to be a dinner? No one has said so, and he is left with the problem of whether or not to have a meal before he goes there.

5. What kind of evening is it to be? Does that vague reference to "new house" mean it is to be a housewarming party? Should he then bring a present? No doubt many people are purposely vague on this point because they don't want the guest to feel he has to bring a present, but if it is a housewarming party it is much better to come straight out and say so, rather than run the risk of some innocent guest turning up to find he is the only one who hasn't brought a gift.

6. Finally there has been no indication of what the guest should wear. Should he turn up in his ordinary suit and risk finding the others in dinner jackets? Or—even more terrible—turn up in his dinner jacket to find the rest in polo-necks and jeans frying sausages in the back garden.

One of the prime purposes of any letter of invitation should be to give enough information to forestall any possible embarrassment to a prospective guest, and on this count alone the above letter fails lamentably.

Keeping all these various points in mind, the letter would have to be rewritten to look something like this:

17, Dunn Street,
Milton.
24, October, 1971.

Dear Harry,

Helen and I are holding a little housewarming party on Thursday, 4th November, and we would be delighted if you could manage to come.

It is a very informal affair, just a few friends, so there will be no need to dress up. Dinner will be around eight o'clock, but if you could come about half an hour earlier it will give us time for a chat and a drink.

We are both looking forward to seeing you very much.

Yours sincerely,
Bill.

An even more tricky invitation to write is the one where you invite a party to come to dinner, and then go on to a dance or a theatre afterwards.

The difficulty is to make sure that the guests understand exactly what the invitation covers and which part, if any, of the expenses they will have to pay themselves.

Let us imagine that the annual golf club dance is coming on. You intend to have a few friends in for dinner and then go on as a party to the dance.

You might send an invitation like this:

Dear John,

We are arranging a small dinner party for Thursday, 17th November, which will then go on to the golf club dance.

We should be very pleased if you could join us.

Dinner will be at 7.30.

Yours sincerely,
James.

This invitation has one great fault. John realises he has been invited to dinner, he realises that he will be going on to the golf club dance afterwards, but what is not quite clear is whether the party is for people who are going to the dance anyway and whether he will be expected to provide his own ticket.

This point should always be made abundantly clear.

If the host intends to pay for everything, the following invitation leaves no room for any doubt.

Dear John,

We are arranging a small party for Thursday, 17th November.

We hope you can come to dinner and then go on with us afterwards as our guest to the golf club dance.

Dress will be formal and dinner will start at 7.30 p.m.

Yours sincerely,
James

49

If the host, on the other hand, wishes the guests to provide their own tickets for the dance, then a letter such as the following will avoid any ambiguity.

Dear John,

As you know next Thursday, 17th November, is the annual golf club dance.

We are having some friends in to dinner beforehand—at 7.30 p.m., to be exact—and if you are intending to go to the dance we'd love to include you in the party.

Any member of the committee will be able to supply you with a ticket, but if you have any difficulty, please let me know and I'll see what I can do.

Yours sincerely,
James.

Exercises

Choose any one of the following letters:

1. Invite a friend to a barbecue you are holding.

2. You have some friends coming who are interested in music. A neighbour, who has recently moved to the district, has similar interests. Invite him to dinner, followed by a musical evening.

3. You have a friend who is playing the leading role in an amateur dramatic production at the local theatre. Invite another friend to have a meal with you, then go on to the theatre afterwards. Make sure that the friend realises you intend to pay for everything.

4. Invite the same friend to a meal followed by the theatre, but make sure the friend realises that you do not intend to buy theatre tickets for everyone.

13

THE FORMAL INVITATION

For informal parties the informal invitation is perfectly adequate. If the party is intended to be extremely formal, however, a formal invitation should be sent.

The formal invitation comes most often in the form of a printed card with a space left blank for the name to be added in handwriting.

The usual form appears below:

Mr and Mrs J. Cunningham
request the pleasure of the company of
Mr and Mrs H. Greene
to Dinner
on Tuesday, 5th March, at 7.30 p.m.

2 Canon Row,
York.   R.S.V.P.

Questions
1. Where does the address appear on this type of letter?
2. It is written in the third person. What does that mean?
3. What does R.S.V.P. stand for?
4. Why is it so important for a reply to be received?

Such a formal invitation requires a formal reply. It is written in the third person in exactly the same style as the invitation.

Mr and Mrs H. Greene thank Mr and Mrs J. Cunningham
for their kind invitation to dinner on Tuesday, 5th March,
and have much pleasure in accepting.

Another form is:

> Mr and Mrs H. Greene accept with pleasure Mr and Mrs J. Cunningham's kind invitation to dinner on Tuesday, 5th March, at 7.30 p.m.

The writer's address, in both cases should be included in the bottom left hand corner.

If the invitation is to be declined instead of accepted, the letter would read as follows:

> Mr and Mrs H. Greene thank Mr and Mrs J. Cunningham for their kind invitation to dinner on Tuesday, 5th March, but regret that owing to a prior engagement they are unable to accept.

It should be noted that the reason for not accepting must be given, and even after that it would be only polite to send a short, informal letter explaining in greater detail why you were prevented from accepting the invitation.

Exercise

Imagine that a friend is holding a formal dinner party. Write a formal invitation to yourself and partner, then compose either a formal acceptance or a formal letter declining the invitation.

14

A STUDY OF THREE LETTERS.

Which One Gets The Job?

In a previous chapter you learned that in any application for a job you must marshal your facts carefully, keep your letter as brief as possible, but at the same time give all the details which are relevant and which will help a prospective employer to judge your suitability.

Below is a typical *Situations Vacant* advertisement and three letters applying for the post advertised.

WANTED—Sales representative for old-established agriculture machinery firm. Apply, giving details of age, education and experience, with the names and addresses of two referees to Personnel Manager, Boyes, Ltd., Barnahill, Norfolk.

---

(1)

Dear Sir,

I wish to apply for the position of sales representative.

I am 21 years of age and was educated at Staneworth Grammar School.

I am employed as a sales representative with Stowes, Ltd.

I would insist on a salary of at least £1,000 per year.

My referees are J. Brown, Esq., 42, Dunleigh Street, Redgray and J. L. Gleeson, Littlehope, Dewruth, Norfolk.

> Yours faithfully,
> James Smith.

Dear Sir,

I wish to apply for the post of sales representative advertised in the current issue of the "Dolmeth Advertiser."

I am twenty years of age and was educated at Dewruth Grammar school, where I took four "A" levels and six "O" levels, including "A" levels in both English and Mathematics.

Since leaving school in 1968 I have been employed by Messrs Steed and Gray, first as a trainee salesman, then later as a salesman in their agricultural branch. I wish to leave now only because the opportunities for promotion are so limited.

My sales manager and my former headmaster have both consented to act as referees. Their addresses are, respectively, A. J. Brown, Esq., Sales Manager, Steed and Gray (Engineering), Southolt, Norfolk and T. Greene, Esq., M.A., The Schoolhouse, Dewruth, Norfolk.

My current salary is £950 per annum, and I should expect a similar starting salary. If, however, you prefer to pay on a salary plus commission basis I am sure this could be arranged to our mutual satisfaction at any interview which you care to arrange.

Yours faithfully,
Alexander Gray.

3

Dear Sir,

I was thrilled to read your advertisement for a sales representative in the "Dolmeth Advertiser", because I can state quite truthfully that it has always been my ambition to work for your firm, which has a justifiably high international reputation for the quality of its products.

I was educated at Barmouth Grammar School, which I left in 1968. My schoolmasters all spoke very highly of my work, and I was always considered the "bright boy" of my class.

I trained for six months as a sales representative with Edgeley Brothers, but I left because their old-fashioned selling methods irked me. I have always been interested in the techniques of selling and, as my father says, could "sell a refrigerator to an Eskimo".

By the way, I won second prize for art in my first year at Barmouth Grammar.

I should expect a fairly high salary, but I will arrange that with you at the interview. I always believe that the workman is worthy of his hire, don't you?

My referees are two of the most respected residents in the district. Their honesty is beyond dispute.

The first is our vicar, Mr Brown. You may have seen him on television on "Late Call", or on one of his many other T.V. appearances. His address is The Vicarage, Barmouth, Norfolk.

My other referee is my scoutmaster, Mr W. Johnstone of 42, Lynmouth Crescent, Barmouth, Norfolk. He has known me almost all my life. I have often been at scout camps with him, where my knowledge of woodcraft proved of great value.

I am sure that if I am given the job you will never regret it, and I look forward confidently to the interview.

Yours faithfully,
Thomas C. Brown.

Questions

1. The advertisement asks specifically for four items of information. Which of the writers has completely ignored the first of these?

2. What criticism could be made of the referees offered by James Smith?

3. Which writer has given the most useful account of his education?

4. Who has given no real estimate of the salary he expects?

5. Who is guilty of the fault of irrelevancy? Quote one example from his letter.

6. Do you consider the details given by James Smith about his experience sufficient for the purpose? If not, what other information would you have liked?

7. Who has marshalled his facts so badly that one piece of information is put in as an afterthought?

8. If you had to judge on the letters alone, to whom would you give the job?

9. Write a short criticism of the other two letters.

Exercise

Carefully avoiding all the faults you have just been criticising, write a letter applying for the following post:

Wanted, clerk (male or female) for postal sales firm. Typing essential. Write in first instance, giving details of age, education, experience and proof of further education since leaving school, together with the names and addresses of two referees to Personnel Officer, Branda, Ltd., Dunmouth, Cumberland.

15

ANSWERING ADVERTISEMENTS

In the average household the advertisements which appear in our newspapers and magazines provide one of the most prolific sources of all letterwriting.

The range is so wide that they offer almost infinite variety. Below is a representative selection:

1. Primo School of Motoring
   Ministry of Transport Approved
   R.A.C. Registered Instructor
   Dual control Austin 1,300 or pupil's own car.
   Proprietor: J. Smith, High Street, Hilltown.

2. Sectional garage for sale, 5 m x 3 m, any reasonable offer accepted. Apply: J. Green, 12, Market Street, Lambhill.

3. Wanted—girl's bicycle to suit 6 to 7 year-old. Cassidy, Lowmore Farm, Barnwood.

4. Cornhill Kennels, dogs and cats boarded, individual runs, resident vet, collection and delivery service if required. Owner: Mrs J. Hillcoat.

5. Rainbow Decorators. All types of painting and decorating. Interior or exterior. First class work. Estimates free. Maurice Cairns, Station Road, Winchampton.

6. Cigarette coupons sold and bought. Reilly, Manor Road, Great Mallington.

The rules for replying to advertisements are the same as for all business letters—brevity, clarity and courtesy.

Everything irrelevant must be avoided, but equally everything that is relevant must be included. It is in deciding what these relevant facts are that the real secret of answering advertisements lies.

In the list of advertisements above, for instance, anyone replying to Advertisement 1 should include the following facts.

(a) Length of course required.

(b) When lessons would be required.

(c) Whether learner will use own car.

(d) Whether learner has already had any instruction.

(e) If learner has already applied for a driving test, and, if so, the date of the test.

The letter should also say whether the learner driver has a provisional licence, and include a request for information on charges.

A reply to the second advertisement might include the following questions:

(a) Whether garage has a wooden floor—or if buyer would have to go to expense of laying a cement one?

(b) Whether seller will make provisions for delivery?

(c) What arrangements there are for viewing?

(d) The age of the garage?

It should also include the price the buyer is willing to pay if the answers to all these questions are satisfactory.

The letter might then look something like this:

Dear Sir,

I was interested in your advertisement in today's "Advertiser" concerning a 5m x 3m garage for sale.

I am anxious to buy such a garage. It must have a wooden floor and be not more than ten years old. The seller would also have to be able to deliver it.

Subject to these conditions being met, and suitable arrangements being made to view the garage, I should be willing to pay £20 for it.

Yours faithfully,
Harold Fulton.

Such a businesslike letter saves the time of both the prospective buyer and the seller. The seller can now tell at a glance whether his garage is suitable, and reply accordingly.

Exercises
Attempt one from each section.
1. Make a list of the points you should include if replying to either Advertisement 3 or Advertisement 4.
2. Write a suitable reply to either Advertisement 5 or Advertisement 6.

16

SET SITUATION—THE WEDDING

One situation in any family which leads to a great deal of letter writing is a wedding.

Even before the wedding takes place several of the letter types which we have studied will have been put into practice.

When the engagement is announced, for instance, there are the letters of congratulations. These are followed by the formal invitations and the formal acceptances or refusals. Finally there are the letters of thanks for the wedding gifts.

The letter of congratulation presents special problems, especially when written to the girl. Custom decrees that the word "congratulations" should be used only when writing to the man, whereas the girl should merely be wished happiness.

A typical congratulatory letter appears below:

Dear Grace,

I have just read the announcement of your engagement to Bill, and I am losing no time in writing to send my best wishes and say how delighted I am to hear it.

I can't say it was a complete surprise, but it is a thrill to get the ring, isn't it? Do come over soon and let me see it.

Yours affectionately,
Sylvia

The formal invitation to the wedding is only slightly different from the one taught in Chapter 13. A typical wedding invitation would look like the one on the facing page.

Mr and Mrs J. Horner
request the pleasure of the company of
Mr and Mrs L. Grant
at the marriage of their daughter
Alice Jean
to
Mr James Allison
at St Mary's Church, Woodfield
on 4th September
at 2.30 p.m.
and afterwards at
Woodfield Hotel

42, Garden Street,   R.S.V.P.
Woodfield.

The thank-you letters for wedding presents cause the same problems as other thank-you letters. You have to say something more than simply "thank you". The difficulty is accentuated in this case because so many thank-you letters are being written at the one time. Most of·the recipients are known to one another and there is the distinct possibility of some of them comparing letters. It is therefore essential to make the letter as personal as possible and to avoid one stereotyped thank-you letter.

A good example appears below.

Dear Aunt Elizabeth,

Thank you very much indeed for your wedding present.

John and I were delighted with the dinner service. It is the only one we have and it looks really magnificent.

Once we move into our new home we hope you will be one of the first to visit us and see for yourself how well it sets off our table.

Yours sincerely,
Helen.

Exercises

Attempt any two of the following:

(a) Write a letter of congratulations to a friend who has just become engaged.

(b) Either accept or turn down a formal invitation to a wedding.

(c) Imagine that you have just received a wedding present from a friend. Write a suitable letter of thanks.

17

REPLYING TO A LETTER

A whole chapter devoted to replying to a letter may seem superfluous, but it is surprising how few people have mastered this simple art.

Long friendly correspondences are conducted, completely ignoring points made in letters received. Others answer a few points and ignore the rest.

Nor are things any better in business correspondence. Below is a typical exchange of business letters:

Dear Sir,

Could you please quote the price for 1 dozen of your Mark V cutting machines and say when delivery could be made.

Yours faithfully,
J. Brown.

Dear Sir,

Thank you for your letter of the 14th August.

The answer to your query is that 1 dozen Mark V cutting machines would cost £560.

Yours faithfully,
A. Smith

It will be noticed immediately that this is not the answer to the customer's query. He is still completely in the dark as to delivery dates.

The simple way of avoiding omissions like this is to have the letter you are answering in front of you. Make notes in the margin if they help. Number the points you wish to reply to, and draw a line through them one by one as you answer them.

Such a method would prevent exchanges like the following, which are so typical of the average friendly correspondence.

Dear Jim,

We were very pleased to hear from you on Tuesday and so excited that you are back in Greyville.

There are so many things we want to ask you.

How is your new job? Is Mr Mathers still foreman? Was Gran surprised to see you? Do the trams still run all the way to Felton Junction?

Uncle Joe was in last night and he was just as interested as the rest of us. He started in the factory, you know, and wonders if the old loading bay is still there, directly in front of the Accounts Section.

Mother sends her love and the enclosed pair of socks. She asks if you'd like a pair of gloves knitted in the same colour, as it is usually very cold up there at this time of the year.

Do write soon—and tell me what you want done about the rabbits. Young Joe is looking after them at the moment, but he will be going off to school next week.

Love,
Mary.

Dear Mary,

Thank you for your letter. It brightened up my day. I have been finding it very boring up here, as I know very few people of my own age.

The weather has not been too good either. It has rained steadily since Friday, and I had to spend most of the weekend sitting in my bedroom looking out at the puddles.

I was pleased to hear that Uncle Joe had looked in. Tell him that not only the old loading bay has gone, but the Accounts Section too. The whole factory has been completely redesigned since his day.

Gran sends her love. She is not as fit as she used to be, but she insists on making me a meal every time I visit her.

Love,
Jim.

P.S. The job isn't too bad although it is inclined to be a bit repetitive.

Exercises

How many questions in Mary's letter does Jim ignore?
Attempt one of the following letters:

1. Rewrite Jim's letter, covering all the questions that Mary asks in hers.
2. A friend has written you a letter informing you, among other things, that his dog has died, that his father has been given promotion in his job, that his sister is to be married soon, and that he himself is considering joining the R.A.F. Reply to his letter, answering the points he makes, and adding a little news of your own.

18

THE LETTER OF COMPLAINT

One letter which requires a great deal of tact is the letter of complaint. The main problem is to state exactly what is in your mind and yet still keep the letter courteous.

Consider the following situation. Your neighbour has a large dog which has taken to coming into your garden. On several occasions you have chased it out, and have even spoken to its owner about it. Now you have returned home from work to discover it has been in again and has dug up a large part of your carefully cultivated vegetable garden.

You feel that this time a letter would have more effect.

You could, of course, write a letter in the following terms.

Dear Jones,

If you don't keep that mangy brute of yours under control I'll put a bullet in it, then come round and wrap the carcase round your fat neck.

Yours faithfully,
A. Smith.

Psychologically this letter might relieve your feelings, but as a letter of complaint it would be a disaster.

In the first place it is unlikely to achieve its effect. The only emotion it can arouse in the recipient is anger, and it would put an end for all time to any neighbourly co-operation.

In the second place there is the legal aspect. The letter has made two threats—one against the dog and one against the owner. There may also be a case against the writer under the heading of libel—the "mangy" dog and the "fat" neck of the owner.

This is an angry letter, and as a general rule the best advice about writing an angry letter can be summed up in one word— don't!

Much more likely to achieve your aim of having the dog kept under proper control is the following letter, which, though courteous, still states your case very fully.

Dear Mr Jones,

I regret to have to inform you that your dog has once again been digging up my garden. An entire bed of spring vegetables, which I planted only last week, has been completely ruined.

As you know, gardening is my one hobby, and I take a special pride in my vegetable garden. Your dog is a very welcome visitor in winter, but I should appreciate it greatly if you could ensure that he is prevented from entering my garden during spring and summer, when there is so much in it that can be damaged.

I trust that this letter causes no offence, and that it in no way affects the friendly relations we have had in the past.

Yours sincerely,

Adam Smith.

Another very common cause of complaints is dissatisfaction with goods bought during shopping.

Let us imagine a typical example.

You have bought an expensive jumper at a local store. The shopkeeper assured you that it was completely pre-shrunk and that it would wash "like a dream". Now the dream has turned into a nightmare. After its first wash the garment has shrunk so badly that it is completely unwearable, and a letter of complaint is obviously in order.

Once again it would no doubt be pleasant to express all your anger and frustration in colourful terms.

You are brimming over with righteous indignation. The more you think about it, the worse it seems. The whole affair is a scandal. That shop assistant should be horsewhipped!

In a towering rage you sit down and compose some such letter as the following:

Dear Sir,

The jumper you sold me last month has shrunk so badly that it would not now fit even a deformed dwarf.

That lying assistant of yours assured me it would wash perfectly.

Unless you return my cash I'll sue you.

Yours faithfully,
Marjorie M. Gray.

Once again, however, the same criticisms can be levelled at it.

The only reaction it is likely to cause is anger, and it leaves the writer open to a very real danger of legal action.

The manager has not yet been given an opportunity to rectify his assistant's mistake. Offer him that opportunity in a restrained, polite letter which places all the facts before him.

Dear Sir,

I bought a jumper in your store towards the end of last month.

The label described it as a "Haston's All-Wool", and your assistant assured me that it was fully shrink-proof. This week—after washing it for the first time very carefully in lukewarm water—it has shrunk so badly that it is now unwearable.

Realising how highly you value the reputation of your shop I am writing to you to bring the matter to your notice, and confidently await your observations.

Yours faithfully,
Marjorie M. Gray.

This is an infinitely better letter of complaint.

It states the facts very clearly, is ready to accept the incident as a rare and untypical mistake, but leaves no doubt at all that if no reply—or an unsatisfactory reply—is received, then the matter will not be allowed to rest there.

Exercises

Attempt one of the following:

1.   The small son of a newly arrived neighbour has just thrown a stone which has smashed a pane of glass in your greenhouse. When you scolded him he became very impertinent. Write a letter of complaint to his father.

2.   A coat which you bought for £25 last month has been completely destroyed by some accident involving fire. The insurance company with which you have dealt for years has just sent you a cheque for £4 as a final settlement of the claim. Complain to the Managing Director of the firm.

3.   A plastic gnome has disappeared from your garden. On your way home you notice one exactly the same in the garden of a house in your neighbourhood. From certain marks on it you are quite sure that it is yours. Write a letter to the occupant of the house insisting on its return.

4.   Imagine that your small son has just arrived home bleeding, bruised and in tears. He informs you that he was set upon by two older boys who live in a house a few streets away. Write a letter to the boys' parents complaining of the incident.

5.   Last session a sum of money went missing from the school. You now learn that a former pupil is spreading the story that you took it. Write a letter of complaint to him firm enough to ensure that the stories stop immediately, but containing nothing that might give him a case for either libel or threats.

19

THE LETTER OF SYMPATHY

This is one of the most difficult of all letters to write.

The recipient is in a highly emotional state.

The writer is torn between the thought that his letter might be an intrusion upon private grief and the risk that, if he does not write, he might be considered hard-hearted and unfeeling.

The contents of the letter present great difficulties too. What can one say at a time like this?

In the past it was the custom to dwell at some length on the virtues of the deceased, but this long formal catalogue tended to lend an air of artificiality to the letter, and the custom has now been largely superseded.

The real secret of the good letter of sympathy is to be natural. There is not much that can be said, but say it simply and sincerely.

Try too to make your letter constructive. If there is any possible help you can give, then offer that help.

A typical letter of sympathy would look something like this:

Dear Tom,

I have just learned your very sad news.

I know that the sympathy of friends cannot lessen grief at a time like this, but I had to write to tell you how deeply I feel for you and how much you are in my thoughts at the moment.

Mary was always such a gentle person. I shall never forget her kindness to me when I lost my own wife.

Please do not bother answering this letter, but when you are feeling a little more able to face the world I do hope you will come down and stay for a few days. You will be more than welcome at any time. A 'phone call is all that is needed.

Yours very sincerely,
John.

A bereavement, of course, is not the only occasion that calls for a letter of sympathy. Other misfortunes, such as a stay in hospital or a serious operation, call for similar treatment.

The approach in this case will, of course, be slightly more cheerful. An attempt should be made to reassure the patient, and a definite promise given—if possible—to visit him.

A suitable letter of sympathy to a person in hospital might read as follows:

Dear Uncle Robert,

I was sorry to learn that you are back in hospital, especially after having been in so recently before.

Aunt Jean informs us that you are in Dr Graham's ward. My next door neighbour was in the same ward only a few months ago and he speaks very highly of him.

When my neighbour went in, he could only move around with the aid of two sticks. Now I often see him striding past on his way to the park, so let's hope Dr Graham has the same success with you.

I understand that visiting on Saturdays is for the full two hours. I hope to see you this Saturday, and I shall save all my news till then.

Yours sincerely,
Edward.

Exercise

Attempt one of the following letters:

Write an imaginary letter of sympathy to

(a) A friend who has just lost one of his parents.

(b) A relative who has been knocked down by a car and is now in hospital.

(c) An elderly former neighbour, about the death of whose wife you have just read in your local paper.

(d) A school friend who has just lost a brother or a sister.

(e) A friend who has just returned from a holiday in Spain, where he ended up in hospital.

(f) The parent of a friend who has been killed in a car crash.

20

THE POSTCARD

Postcards come in two distinct varieties:

(a) The plain (or business) postcard.

(b) The picture postcard.

The purposes for which the two types are intended are so different that they must be treated as two completely separate categories.

The Plain (or Business Postcard)

The plain postcard is basically a simplified letter. On the one side it has a place for the address. The other side is completely blank and is intended for the letter.

It has certain basic advantages:

(a) It saves time. There is no need to find an envelope, put the letter into it and seal it up. At first sight the time saving may seem minor, but it can be considerable when a great many messages have to be sent out, e.g. when summoning a number of people to a meeting.

(b) Being of uniform size, they are very easily filed. So easily handled are they, in fact, that many firms specify a postcard in their advertisements.

(c) They were formerly cheaper to post, but this has been changed recently and that advantage has, for the time being at least, now disappeared.

They have also certain built-in disadvantages:

(a) The message must of necessity be short.

(b) It must also be one that you do not wish to keep private, as it will be there for anyone to read throughout its entire journey.

The illustrations show

(a) The address side of a business postcard.

(b) A typical message that might be sent on one.

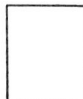

POST CARD
THE ADDRESS TO BE WRITTEN ON THIS SIDE

R. Broome, Esq,
17, Landbrooke Crescent,
Granville,
Somerset.

Klanklax Ltd,
14, High Street,
Marton.
14th November, 1971.

Dear Sir,

Thank you for your enquiry.

Our representative will call on Tuesday morning at 10 a.m. to demonstrate our latest model.

Yours faithfully,
J. Greene
(Sales Manager)

The Picture Postcard

The picture postcard is associated almost exclusively with holidays. It is an attempt to share a little of the pleasure of the holiday with those left behind at home.

On one side is a picture of the resort to give the recipient some idea of its beauty. The other side is divided in two, leaving one half for the address and one half for a short message.

The reverse side of a typical picture postcard is shown over.

73

```
          POST  CARD              ┌──────┐
                                  │      │
                                  │      │
Having a                         └──────┘
wonderful time here.
Weather perfect.          Mr. J. Gibson,
Wish you were here.          32, Hillcrest View,
        Joe                     Heathill,
                                  Sussex.
```

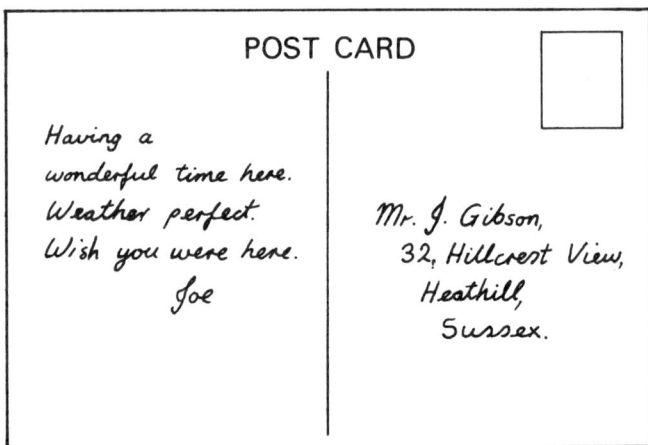

It will be noticed that the greeting (or salutation) and the ending are both dispensed with in the picture postcard.

It will also be noticed that the average postcard is written in a strange kind of shorthand, full of trite and hackneyed phrases. This is a pity, since the postcard repays careful composition just as much as the letter.

A slightly more ambitious example appears below:

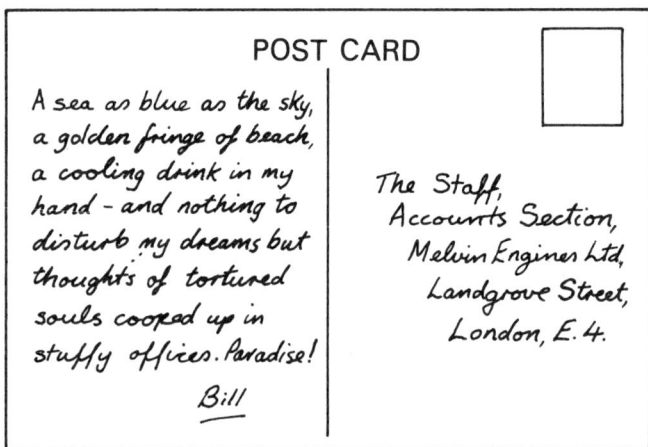

```
          POST  CARD              ┌──────┐
                                  │      │
A sea as blue as the sky,         └──────┘
a golden fringe of beach,
a cooling drink in my
hand - and nothing to      The Staff,
disturb my dreams but         Accounts Section,
thoughts of tortured           Melvin Engines Ltd,
souls cooped up in              Landgrove Street,
stuffy offices. Paradise!        London, E. 4.
        Bill
```

There is also great scope for verse, as in this humorous post-card from a holidaymaker in France to his friend in Scotland.

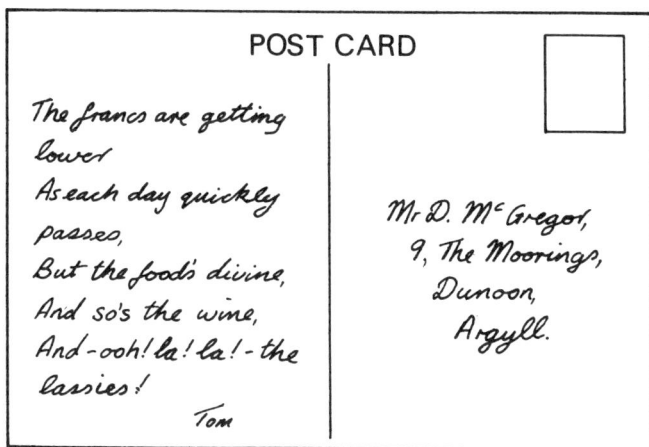

```
┌─────────────────────────────────────────────────┐
│                POST CARD          ┌──────────┐   │
│                              │    │          │   │
│  The francs are getting      │    │          │   │
│  lower                       │    └──────────┘   │
│  As each day quickly         │                   │
│  passes,                     │   Mr D. McGregor, │
│  But the food's divine,      │    9, The Moorings,│
│  And so's the wine,          │      Dunoon,      │
│  And-ooh! la! la!-the        │      Argyll.      │
│  lassies!                    │                   │
│              Tom             │                   │
└─────────────────────────────────────────────────┘
```

Exercises

Attempt any one of the following:

    (a) Draw the two sides of a business postcard. On one side put the address of your local T.V. repair service. On the other write a message informing him that you are having trouble with your T.V. set and giving a choice of dates when you would like their mechanic to call.

    (b) Draw the reverse side of a picture postcard. Address it to a friend, then write a light-hearted message in either prose or verse.

21

THE LETTER OF APOLOGY (PERSONAL)

If there is one letter that is more difficult to write than the letter of complaint it is the letter of apology.

In the letter of complaint you have your own sense of outraged innocence to sustain you. In the letter of apology all you have is a sense of guilt.

Just how abject the apology should be depends on the magnitude of the offence.

The good letter of apology should also be constructive. If there has been a mistake made, then a full explanation should be given as to how it came to be made. If damage has been sustained, then an offer should be made to put right this damage as far as it is within the writer's power to do so.

Above all the letter must be courteous and ungrudging. The sole aim is to conciliate, and the letter of apology that does not conciliate is better left unwritten.

Consider the following situation:

You have a small son who has just confessed to you tearfully that he has kicked his football through a neighbour's window. It is only a month since he kicked the same ball through exactly the same window. An immediate letter of apology is required, and might be written as follows:

Dear Mrs Dawson,

I was most upset to learn that Tommy had kicked his ball through your sitting room window again this afternoon.

He has been warned repeatedly not to play football on that piece of waste ground beside your house, especially since the last incident. Unfortunately he disobeyed me, and I can only offer my sincere apologies.

When you have the window repaired, please send the bill to me. I intend to keep the money out of Tommy's pocket money in the hope that this will teach him a lesson.

Apologising once again,

> I remain,
>> Yours sincerely.
>>> Alice Greene.

This letter is a good example of the three golden rules of the letter of apology:

(a) Conciliation
(b) Explanation
(c) Reparation

Now let us examine a slightly more serious situation.

After a party at your house it is discovered that one of your records—a new one—is missing. A certain guest has admired it all evening, asking for it to be played again and again.

You suspect him, and the following day accuse him in an angry scene in front of two or three people of having stolen the record.

When you return home you discover the record under a book. You now have the unenviable job of writing a letter of apology.

The rules are exactly the same as for all letters of apology.

Under *"Conciliation"*, however, it should be realised that the apology in this case must be much more abject. This is no minor matter like a broken window. A person's character has been defamed completely unjustifiably. If he cares to take the matter to court there is not the shadow of a doubt that he would win his case.

The *"Explanation"* too must appear a little thin, but there is no other course but to offer it as honestly and as diplomatically as possible.

The *"Reparation"* is very difficult also. All that can be offered is a sincere attempt to repair as much of the damage you have caused as possible.

Dear Jim,

Can you ever forgive me for my completely indefensible conduct this afternoon?

My only excuse—a very poor one—is that I prized the record so much that my anger at its disappearance made me lose all sense of proportion. The fact that you admired it as well became in my heated imagination a reason for suspecting you.

I now realise how completely unjust and unfounded this was. I have found the record and have been suffering agonies of remorse ever since.

I've been round to see Tom and Bill and I have explained the whole matter to them. If you think that anyone else heard my outburst I shall be only too grateful for the opportunity of giving them a full explanation as well.

I know it is a great deal to ask, but I hope that my unforgivable stupidity hasn't ruined our friendship for all time. Do come round for a cup of coffee tomorrow evening to let me apologise personally and try to make up in some small measure for the hurt I have caused you.

Yours in great distress,
Bill.

Exercises

Attempt any one of the following:

1. In Chapter 18 we had a situation where an Alsatian had dug up a newly planted vegetable plot in a neighbour's garden. The neighbour wrote a polite letter of complaint. Imagine that it was your dog which caused the damage and write a letter of apology.

2. Your neighbour has gone on holiday for a month. He left you his garage and car keys and asked if you would occasionally run his engine to keep his battery from going flat. The first time you did this you didn't notice his car was in gear until it lurched forward violently, damaging not only the car but the garage as well. Write a letter of apology to your neighbour at his holiday address.

3. A friend has sent you some foreign stamps, which he has just received, because you have a catalogue, and he wishes to know how valuable they are. Some accident has happened to the stamps when they are in your care and they have been completely destroyed. Apologise to him for your carelessness.

4. You have heard that someone has been telling tales about you. You challenge him, but he denies it. You roundly berate him for everything from cowardice to infamy. The following day you discover the culprit was another person with the same name. Write and apologise.

5. You have been digging the foundations for an ornamental pool in your garden. One evening an elderly neighbour, returning the garden shears which he has borrowed, falls into the hole. Write to him in hospital and apologise for the accident.

22

WHAT'S WRONG WITH THESE LETTERS?

Throughout this book the three basic ingredients of a good business letter—brevity, clarity and courtesty—have been continually stressed.

There is one other essential ingredient—common sense.

Below is a collection of business letters which show just how often this ingredient is lacking:

Letter A

17, Acacia Villas.
18th Sept., 1971.

Dear Sir,
Will you please send me a copy of your recent catologue.

Yours faithfully,
Albert Bloggs.

Question:
What essential information has been omitted?

Letter B

13, Dead End Lane,
Kidmore,
Bucks.
14th August, 1972.

Dear Sir,
I should like to enquire if you are likely to have a vacancy in your firm. I am at present working for the B.B.C., but I want a job nearer home.

Yours truly,
E. A. Smith.

Questions:

1. Is the writer a man or a woman?
2. What does the writer do?
3. What are the writer's qualifications?
4. Does such a letter really justify a reply from a prospective employer?

Letter C

1A Grand Mansions,
Albert Road,
Leeds.
14th May, 1971.

To the Lost Property Office,
Leeds Central Station.

Dear Sir,

I left an umbrella in a train last Friday. Would you please let me know if you have found it.

Yours faithfully,
J. Frame.

Questions:

1. On which train was it left?
2. Is it a man's or a woman's umbrella?
3. What colour is it?

Letter D

The Vicarage,
Thames Side Road,
Surbiton.
14th December, 1971.

The Black Machine Tool Company Ltd.,
Harlow,
Essex.

Dear Sir,

Recently I purchased one of your Mark V power drills. I was drilling a hole in my bedroom wall, in order to fix a bracket on the wall, when suddenly the drill stopped.

Would you please tell me what is wrong with it? I have had it only six months and it is still under guarantee.

Yours faithfully,
W. Galsworthy.

Questions:

1. Has the writer given the tool company enough information to enable them to answer his enquiry?
2. What would the tool company really require before they could answer the query?

Correspondence E

This is a series of letters which passed between a manufacturer and a printing company.

From a manufacturer to a printer:

The Crown Printing Co.,
Headstone Lane,   22nd September, 1971.
Huddersfield.

Dear Sirs,
Your promised delivery date for supply of our catalogues was 20th September.
This is to inform you that we have not yet received delivery and our Autumn sales programme will be seriously affected if we do not receive these catalogues within the next three days.
Please treat this matter as urgent.

Yours faithfully,

From the Crown Printer Co. to the Manufacturer:

24th September, 1971.

Dear Sirs,
We are replying to your letter of 22nd September, concerning your catalogues. Unfortunately the delay is due to a query we sent you on 10th September, on page 8 of your corrected proofs, to which we have not received a reply. As soon as we have your answer to this query, we will proceed as quickly as possible with the printing.

Yours faithfully,

To the Crown Printing Co. from the Manufacturer:

26th September, 1971.

Dear Sirs,

Thank you for your letter of 24th September, concerning our catalogue.

We cannot trace receiving your letter of 10th September. May we have a copy? The matter is really most urgent.

Yours faithfully,

From the Crown Printer:

28th September, 1971.

Dear Sirs,

We enclose a copy of our letter of 10th September.

Yours faithfully,

From the Manufacturer:

30th September, 1971.

Dear Sirs,

Thank you for your letter. We are quite unable to answer the query you raise without reference to the proofs themselves. It would have saved valuable time if you had anticipated this. Please send the proofs.

Comment:

Correspondence like this, exasperating and timewasting, is not an infrequent occurrence in offices.

A telephone call might have solved this problem more easily, but the printer could have helped greatly if in his first letter he had enclosed both his original query and the proofs.

Exercises

Correct Letters A to D, putting in all the details you feel are essential, then in Correspondence E re-write the printer's first letter in such a way as to make all the rest of the correspondence unnecessary.

23

LETTERS TO THE EDITOR

Almost every newspaper and periodical has a section where readers can air their own views.

Many encourage readers to comment on articles which have appeared in previous issues. Others encourage television criticism or chatty little letters detailing some humorous event which has happened to the writer. Others again prefer serious letters on local or national issues.

There are, in short, about as many different kinds of letters as there are newspapers.

It is also one of the most rewarding types of letter writing.

There is the unique chance to air your views to a wide reader-ship. There is the bonus of seeing your own name in print. Many newspapers also pay a small fee for the privilege of using your letter.

Nor are the rules for the successful letter to the editor very different from the rules for the successful business letter.

The main point for both is to remember that the man to whom you are writing is a very busy person who handles a great deal of correspondence. It is therefore essential to keep your letter short.

You may send to the editor six closely written pages of impeccable prose, full of carefully reasoned argument, making all your points lucidly and strikingly—but one thing is certain. It will never be published. What the editor is looking for is a variety of viewpoints, and he will most certainly never hand over his entire "Letters to the Editor" column to you.

The other fault which all editors abhor is dullness. No matter how uninteresting your letter to a friend may be he will plough through it simply because it comes from you. Not so the reader of a newspaper. He will read the first line, and if it doesn't interest him he will immediately move on to something else.

It is therefore essential to find the eye-catching or memorable phrase—especially in your opening lines. Your points must be made pithily and strikingly. There is absolutely no room for meaningless padding.

Let us look at a few examples.

Take, for instance, the imaginary case of a local council which has decided to develop as a cemetery a piece of waste ground in the middle of a council housing estate.

A local resident might write thus:

Dear Sir,

I object to the latest proposal of the council. Speaking as one who lives in the area I feel the outlook from the council flats will be spoiled completely. I do not feel either that it is a very suitable atmosphere in which to bring up our children.

I consider that developing the area as a children's playpark would be a much more acceptable idea.

Yours faithfully,
John Ellis.

This letter has one main fault.

It completely lacks impact. With such an explosive subject the writer still fails to get across to the reader his burning indignation. He hasn't even outlined the terrible proposal to which he is objecting, and the whole letter lacks the force and pithiness which will make an editor choose it from the twenty or so he is almost certain to receive on the same subject.

Much more likely to be published is the one below.

Dear Sir,

What are they feeding our councillors on these days—bats' blood?

Never in my life have I heard anything quite so gruesome as

their proposal to site the new cemetery right in the centre of the new housing estate.

There must surely be—if only for the sanity of the flatdwellers there—some slightly more imaginative use, such as a children's playground, to which the piece of ground can be put.

Yours faithfully,
Harold Jones.

Now let us look at an example of T.V. criticism.

Dear Sir,

I found John Timmin's programme "Songs I Have Loved" very dull. His last number especially—"I Beg Your Pardon"—was poorly sung.

I feel we could have much brighter programmes.

Yours faithfully,
E. Richards.

Once again this letter has only one real fault. It lacks impact. It degenerates into a series of trite complaints.

If the writer had thought a little he would have realised immediately that he had a golden opportunity for a bright, humorous opening with a pun on his complaint about the song "I Beg Your Pardon".

Rearranged a little his letter would become:

Dear Sir,

I note that John Timmin's final number last week was "I Beg Your Pardon".

At least it's some consolation that he had the decency to

apologise for the boredom we've suffered week after week with his series, "Songs I Have Loved".

Surely our programme planners can do a little better than this.

Yours faithfully,
E. Richards.

Finally there is the other type of letter to the editor—the chatty little story about some humorous event that has happened to the writer.

Usually these come in cycles. One reader writes in about an amusing remark made by his four-year-old son, and for weeks afterwards the readers' letters columns in that paper are full of letters from proud parents relating the smart sayings of their own four-year-olds.

Imagine, in this case, that the subject of the correspondence is "doubles". Someone has remarked that a famous sporting personality is the double of a famous film star. This has started a spate of letters on striking likenesses.

A reader might write thus:

Dear Sir,

I agree with your correspondent last week that everyone has a double somewhere.

My own incident happened at London Airport when I was approached by a strange woman who greeted me warmly as "Hugo". She apologised almost immediately, but remarked that I was "Hugo's double".

Tempted, I stayed on in the hope of seeing this person who was so like me.

When he turned up, however, he didn't resemble me in the slightest.

Yours faithfully,
Ernest Longton.

The most that can be said for this letter is that it is on the subject of "doubles". It is a trite little tale, and any editor who used it would have to be very hard up for material.

Let us add a little humour to it, tell it a little more dramatically, and see what happens.

Dear Sir,

I agree with your correspondent last week that everyone has a double.

Standing in London Airport recently I was approached by a strange woman and greeted warmly as "Hugo".

When she realised her mistake and apologised it should have been my signal to go, but it is not every day we have the chance to see ourselves as others see us—so I waited.

Sure enough, she started "Hugo-ing" all over the airport again.

I looked at the man she was approaching and immediately recognised my own jutting chin. There was something in his manly gait too which recalled mine, and his forelock curled over his forehead in that attractive way I have so often noticed in my own mirror.

In fact, I had just reached the stage of recognising how forgivable her earlier mistake had been, when a terrible thing happened.

She ran right past the handsome stranger and threw herself into the arms of an insignificant, pigeon-chested, balding creature in horn-rimmed spectacles and an ill-fitting serge suit!

Yours faithfully,
Ernest Longton.

The same incident—but what a world of difference between the two letters. A little care in the construction, a little imagination, a little humour—and you have transformed a dull little letter into one that is really worth receiving.

The following is a collection of actual letters from the press, which will show you the vast scope of such letters.

Legal Advice
Dear Sir,

Our London hotel failed to give us the early call we ordered and we missed our charter flight. We were charged extra and sent on a scheduled flight. Can we sue the hotel?

Yours faithfully,
Henry Brown.

Anecdote
Dear Sir,

The science teacher at my son's school had just given a lesson to show that carbon dioxide turns lime water milky. To prove his point he breathed into a bottle of limewater and immediately the carbon dioxide in his breath turned it milkwhite.

"Any questions?", he asked.

Amid an awed silence one pupil put up his hand.

"Please, sir," he asked admiringly, "will anybody's breath do that?"

Yours etc.

Politics
Dear Sir,

How can the government penny-pinch on school milk supplies and put the health of this country back fifty years?

Yours etc.

Philosophy
Dear Sir,

Have you ever noticed how inconsistent parents are?

Mother scolds me for talking at table, then talks non-stop herself throughout the meal.

Dad warns me about misbehaving at school, then regales the company proudly with hilarious tales of the mischief he got up to in his own schooldays.

Yours etc.

91

Shopping Advice
Dear Sir,

My problem is that I am a woman who takes size 9 shoes. Try as I might I cannot find a stockist in the Birmingham area. Can you or any of your readers help me?

Yours etc.

Medical Advice
Dear Sir,

My husband, who is 55, is continually complaining of tiredness. He is also very forgetful.

Could it be anaemia or an early warning of heart disease?

Yours etc.

Cosmetic Problems
Dear Sir,

I cannot wear eye make-up because the skin around my eyes is very sensitive. Can you recommend a suitable make-up?

Yours etc.

Complaint
Dear Sir,

After a holiday spent touring Britain I must really complain of the service we are offered everywhere in this country. Why can't we have waiters of the same standard as those on the Continent?

A few more catering schools would work wonders for our tourist industry.

Yours etc.

Affairs Of The Heart
Dear Sir,

My problem is I cannot get a steady girl friend. The good-looking ones I fancy don't fancy me. There is one in particular who travels to work on my train every morning. What can I do to make her notice me?

Yours etc.

Comment On Previous Articles
Dear Sir,

I did enjoy John Grinley's article on the Shetlands. His descriptions were magnificent and vividly recalled for me the landscape among which I spent my childhood.

Yours etc.

Injustices
Dear Sir,

Which superior male mind first invented women's hankies? We have as big noses as men. We are as likely to catch cold as men. Yet what are we offered? A postage stamp size scrap of lace that is about as useful as a set of reins in a modern space craft.

Yours etc.

Argument
Dear Sir,

Why do football pools still continue to give such huge dividends? I am sure most people would like a much greater number of smaller prizes.

Yours etc.

Dear Sir,

Why tamper with our football pools? It is the only hope most of us have of making the "rags to riches" dream come true.

Yours etc.

Exercises

Choose one of the following letters:

1. In your local paper there have been several letters recently about whether or not the Queen requires a pay rise. Write a letter—signed Royalist—backing the Queen's right to an increase. Alternatively write a letter—signed Realist—taking the opposite view.

2. Write—in the style of the second letter on "doubles"—a letter relating some humorous incident which has happened to you.

3. A local councillor has criticised a large industrial project which is to be built in your area, because—as he claims—it would disturb seagulls during the breeding season. You are more concerned with the jobs the project will bring to an area where more than 20,000 are out of work. Write a letter to your local editor beginning "Strictly for the birds! That seems to be the view that Councillor Smith takes of our district........"

24

HOW TO SAY "NO"

One of the most difficult things to say in a letter is the simple word "No".

Even with an invitation to tea it is much easier to phrase a reply accepting the invitation than to write one turning it down.

There are also many more difficult occasions on which a refusal is necessary.

Take, for example, the request by a friend for a loan. Granting the loan would present no problems. Writing a letter refusing the loan, yet avoiding hurting your friend's feelings is a much more difficult matter.

Some such letter as the following would be necessary:

Dear Jim,

I was extremely sorry to hear of your run of bad luck and the financial mess in which it has left you.

Remembering all your kindnesses in the past I should have been only too pleased to give you any help I could. Unfortunately there is one serious drawback. I too have had a series of expenses, and I just don't have £50 at the moment.

I do hope that you manage to overcome your problems, and forgive me once again for being unable to help.

Yours sincerely,
Ted.

Just as difficult as a loan to turn down is an unwanted honour. A friend, for example, may wish you to be his best man. In such a case, if no cast-iron excuse is available, a very good one must be invented.

Dear Bill,

I was delighted to learn that you are to be married next month and thrilled that you should have thought of me for your best man.

Unfortunately I must decline the honour. I shall be out of the country at the time. My boss is sending me on a selling trip to Europe, and, much as I should like to, I just can't refuse.

With your wide circle of friends, however, I have no doubt you will be able to find a replacement at least as suitable as myself.

Give my best wishes to Jean and assure her that I'll be thinking of you both very fondly on the big day.

Apologising once again for being unable to accept.

I remain,
Yours sincerely,
David.

This letter would probably be a little short for the purpose, but it does give some idea of how the bitter pill of refusal must be coated fairly liberally with the sugar of friendly flattery.

Not all unwanted honours, of course, come from friends. Organisations are also guilty in this respect. Although for them the bitter pill of refusal must be sugared too, it should be sugared just a little more formally.

Dear Mr Jenkins,

Thank you for your letter of the 14th August in which you informed me that my name had been suggested for the vice-presidency of the club.

I am deeply conscious of the honour being done me, but unfortunately I must decline. I am in my final year at university this session, and I feel that my studies would prevent me from devoting all the time and the energy to the post which it merits.

I trust that you will convey my thanks to the Committee and explain my position to them.

Yours sincerely,
John Edwards.

Exercises

Attempt one of the following letters:

(a) A friend has written, suggesting you should both go on holiday together this year. You know that you would be absolutely bored. Write a letter, politely declining the suggestion.

(b) An acquaintance has offered you a share in a new business venture. You could afford the very small sum necessary to start the enterprise, but you do not want to take the risk. Write and turn down the offer.

(c) The secretary of your local Woman's Guild has written, asking if you would give a talk to her members on your recent trip to Iceland. Refuse the invitation.

25

THE LETTER OF RESIGNATION

The letter of resignation is one that is very often associated in people's minds with the elderly.

This is a misconception. Even the very young may be members of clubs, committees, youth fellowships, etc., and could face the necessity for resigning at any time and for any one of a variety of reasons.

The letter of resignation should always be short. It should contain the formal announcement of your resignation, the date from which it will take effect and your reason for resigning. If the parting has been amicable it might also include a very brief appreciation of any kindness or services you have received in the past.

The following is a typical example:

Dear Sir,

Since I am leaving the district at the end of August I wish to give notice of my intention of resigning from the post of club secretary on that date.

At the same time I should like to record my appreciation of the loyal support I have received from club members during my term of office, and to add my good wishes for the continuing success of the club.

Yours faithfully,
Edgar Grant.

Occasionally, however, the parting is not quite so amicable. Disputes break out on even the best-conducted committees, and sometimes the disputes become too frequent to be ignored.

In that case a slightly different letter of resignation would be required:

Dear Sir,

For some time now I have been aware of a clash of personalities on the committee.

This is not in the best interests of the club, and I feel the simplest solution would be for me to step down from the office of Vice President.

I accordingly tender my resignation with effect from Friday, 14th June.

Yours faithfully,
Henry Williams.

When the resignation is not from a club, but from a job, the problem is slightly different. Most firms have as part of their contract a certain minimum notice they require of any employee's intention to resign. It should be made abundantly clear in your letter that it is this statutory notice which you are giving them.

A typical letter of resignation would read as follows:

Dear Sir,

As I am emigrating to Australia next month I wish to give the statutory four weeks' notice of my intention of resigning from my post as clerk with this firm on Friday, 12th November.

Yours faithfully,
Paul Gray.

Exercises

Write a letter of resignation for one of the following:

(a) The captain of a tennis club, who feels that since he has gone to university he cannot devote sufficient time to the club.

(b) The secretary of a social club, who can no longer stand the president's continual interference with his duties.

(c) A junior clerk, who has just been offered a better job with another firm.

(d) The captain of a badminton club, who has just been advised by his doctor to give up the game.

26

THE PEN PAL

One modern institution which gives rise to a great many letters is the "pen pal".

All kinds of organisations, from schools to newspapers and magazines, are willing to arrange these pen friendships. As the aim is usually international understanding the writers generally come from different countries.

This leads to certain language difficulties. Although, with foreign language correspondents, each writer usually writes in his own language, it should be remembered that to the recipient it is a foreign tongue, and all slang should be carefully avoided.

With pen pals from other English-speaking countries the same care should be taken. Every country adds its own flavour to the English language. Tell an American, for instance, that you have gas in your flat and he'll wonder how you got petrol in your puncture, so care must be taken to keep your language as simple and uncomplicated as possible.

Another important feature of the pen friendship is that this is a friend you are unlikely ever to meet. You will get to know each other through your letters alone. They are your only ambassadors, and should be given all the respect and care that such ambassadors deserve.

These are the disadvantages, but the pen pal letter has advantages too.

One of the main advantages lies in your subject matter. Details which may appear trite and mundane to you will, to your pen pal, seem quaint and exotic, and this should always be remembered when writing the letter.

Examine the following example, written to a Continental pen pal.

Linden Lea,
Hargrove,
Wilts.
24th December, 1971.

Dear Anne-Marie,

As you will see from the date I am writing this on Christmas Eve. It is growing dark, and the snow is beginning to fall, so we are almost certain of a white Christmas.

In a few hours it will be time to join the Church Youth Fellowship group on their choir-singing round of the village. At about 10 p.m. we shall finish at our local hospital, where a cup of tea and sandwiches will be waiting for us.

By then it will almost be time to join the rest of the village in church for the Christmas Eve service. By the time we come back out into the snow it will be Christmas Day. Dad will probably invite a few neighbours in for a drink, but we shall all be in bed by 2 a.m., for tomorrow morning we must all be up early to open our presents, which are stacked at the moment in neat piles under the Christmas tree.

After we receive our presents I shall be helping mother to prepare the Christmas meal. It is a very traditional one, turkey followed by Christmas pudding, over which father will pour some of his precious brandy and ceremoniously set it alight.

Since father is the eldest brother most of our family collect in our house for Christmas. Uncle Harry, who lives in York, has already arrived by train, and will stay overnight. Uncle Joe and Aunt Mary will walk over from their farm. Uncle Peter and Aunt Helen will motor in from Grantford.

After the meal the adults will re-fill their glasses, and we shall all settle down in front of the television set to listen to the Queen's speech.

I am looking forward to it all very much, and I hope that you have just as happy a Christmas. Do write and tell me about it.

Yours sincerely,
Anna.

102

To a British reader the letter may merely describe the normal Christmas scene which we all know so well, but to a Continental reader it has all the quaint charm of unusual customs.

Exercises

Attempt one of the following:

(a) You are spending a typical seaside holiday in this country. Write to your Continental pen friend about it.

(b) Describe your life at school to your American pen friend, stressing in particular those aspects of it which make it different from an American school, e.g. uniform, sports, subjects, etc.

(c) It is a wet Sunday in your town or village. Almost everything is closed. Conjure up a little of the misery of it for a Continental pen pal who is used to Sunday being the gayest day of the week.

27

THE MORE AMBITIOUS PERSONAL LETTER— THE LONGER LETTER

The technique of the longer letter is very little different from that of any other letter. It is merely that it has to be sustained longer.

A little more orderliness of thought is required. A little more care with the paragraphing is needed.

A very good idea is to make a plan of your paragraphs before you begin your letter.

Let us look at an actual example.

In the pen pal letters mentioned in the last chapter your pen pal has written his first letter to you, and has described his life up till then. It is now your turn to reply and do the same.

Your paragraph plan might look like this:

1. Thanks for letter and comments
2. Age, family and house
   (a) Father
   (b) Mother
   (c) Brother
3. Where born
4. Where you live now
5. School
6. Hobbies
   (a) Sport
   (b) Stamp collecting
   (c) Music
7. Where you spend holidays
8. Concluding paragraph to round off letter.

The letter would look something like this:

Dear Hans,

Thank you very much for your letter and the photographs, which I was delighted to receive. Your family looks very nice, and, to my eyes at least, your house seems huge.

Like you I am fifteen years of age, and I too have only one brother. We live in a three-bedroomed house in the town of Gransport, about 80 miles from London.

My father, who is 45, is a schoolteacher. He has taught primary subjects all his life and is now headmaster of our local primary school. He is also a very keen sportsman, and is the current champion of the town golf club.

My mother is the same age as my father. They were in the same class at school and have known each other all their lives. She is the gardener of the family, and takes a special pride in our rose garden.

Tom, my brother, is four years younger than I am. He attends my father's school, but does not like it, as he feels that father is a bit hard on him. He is not very keen on lessons, and I think that my father tries very hard to make a scholar out of him.

Although we now live in Gransport it is only two years since we moved here. I was born in a little village in the Cotswolds, one of the most beautiful parts of England. It was a very friendly village—everyone knew everyone else—and we all adored it. However, promotion took my father to Gransport, and we all had to move here.

Gransport is a rather grimy port and market town with about 50,000 inhabitants . . .

The letter has been left deliberately unfinished, but it gives a good idea of how a well-constructed letter can be built up on the framework of your original paragraph plan.

Exercises

Attempt any one of the following:

   (a) Write a letter similar to the one in this chapter, telling your life story to a new pen pal.

   (b) Imagine that you have just moved house. In a letter describe your new village or town to a friend who has never seen it.

   (c) You have just received a letter from someone you haven't seen since you were seven years old. Write a long letter, bringing him up to date with all that has happened to you since then.

28

ANCIENT AND MODERN

The principles of a good modern business style have been stressed throughout this book. Letters should be clear, concise and straightforward.

Some of our more conservative firms, however, still cling to an older business style, and it is as well to know a little about these older-fashioned business methods.

Business letters were formerly much more formal and flowery. They employed a wordy jargon completely unlike everyday language.

"I received" became "I am in receipt of", "a letter" turned into "an esteemed favour", "tell" became "advise", "immediately" "forthwith", and "to write" "to communicate with".

They used such circumlocutions as "I beg to inform you" and "I wish to state" instead of getting on with the actual job of informing or stating.

They also employed a whole host of complicated abbreviations, such as "inst." (this month), "ult." (last month)) and "prox" (next month).

Other favourites included such phrases as:
Enclosed please find (I enclose)
Yours to hand (I have received your letter)
Of even date (today's date)
Hereafter and henceforth (from now on)
Due to the fact that (because)
In due course (soon)
Yours of recent date (your recent letter)

A typical, old-style business correspondence would look something like that on the following pages.

Brown and Kelly, Ltd.,
High Street,
Taunton.
14th January, 1938.

J. Martin, Esq.,
Stationer,
Garden Terrace,
Newlyn.

Dear Sir,

Enclosed herewith please find our catalogue for the year 1938.

Thanking you for past favours and assuring you of our best attention at all times.

I beg to remain, sir,
Your obedient servant,
John Connelly.

Garden Terrace,
Newlyn.
29th January, 1938.

John Connelly, Esq.,
Brown & Kelly, Ltd.,
High Street,
Taunton.

Dear Sir,

With reference to your esteemed favour of the 17th inst. I am now in receipt of your current catalogue and wish to thank you for same.

Please find enclosed our order for two dozen of your best fountain pens. Kindly advise forthwith as to the expected date of delivery.

I have the honour to be, sir,
Yours faithfully,
J. Martin.

Brown and Kelly, Ltd.,
High Street,
Taunton.
30th January, 1938.

J. Martin, Esq.,
Stationer,
Garden Terrace,
Newlyn.

Dear Sir,
Yours of yesterday's date is now to hand.
I beg to acknowledge receipt of your esteemed order for two dozen of our best fountain pens (catalogue No 1464).
I further beg leave to advise that the goods will be delivered to your premises on the 5th prox.
Awaiting the favour of your continued patronage,

I remain, sir,
Your obedient servant,
John Connelly.

Exercises

1. Rewrite the old-fashioned correspondence in this chapter as you think two modern firms would conduct it.
You might begin:

Dear Sir,
I enclose our 1972 catalogue.
Thank you for past custom.

Yours faithfully,
John Connelly.

2. Put into old-fashioned business English the following letter:

Dear Sir,

Thank you for your letter of 17th August, enclosing order for one gross pencil sharpeners.

We regret that this item is now out of stock, but will write immediately further supplies are available.

Yours sincerely,
James Smith.

THE SET SITUATION—THE CLUB SECRETARY

One situation which involves young people in considerable correspondence is the simple act of joining a club.

Even as an ordinary member there are such things as the letter of application or the covering note along with your annual subscription, but the real bulk of correspondence comes if you are elected to the post of secretary or treasurer. Very soon you will find yourself faced with the whole range of correspondence we have been discussing, together with many others concerned with the day-to-day running of the club.

Once again the same rule applies as for all business correspondence—a brief, courteous letter, giving all relevant facts.

A request to members for their annual subscriptions, for instance, might look like this:–

Dear Sir,

At a recent meeting of the committee it was decided that the membership fee will once again be £3.50 this year.

All subscriptions are now due.

Yours, etc.

Such a letter, once composed, could be duplicated, and thus save much clerical work.

Other letters are not quite so straightforward. One of the most difficult is the letter to a member who is late with his subscription. Great care must be taken to avoid giving offence, yet the writer must never lose sight of the main point—the request for money.

Dear Mr Brown,

On looking over our accounts for this year we discover that your annual subscription has not yet been paid.

We realise, of course, that this must have been an oversight, but since we are now anxious to complete our accounts for the year we should appreciate it if you could send on your remittance at your earliest convenience.

Yours, etc.

Exercises

1. Write a formal invitation, inviting a member and his partner, to your club's annual dinner dance

or

Answer such a formal invitation on behalf of yourself and partner

or

Write an informal invitation to a former member, who is back in the district on holiday, inviting him to a club social.

2. A supplier has promised to deliver goods in time for an important event in your club. You now discover that a week after he promised delivery, and only four days before the event, the goods haven't arrived. Write a letter of complaint

or

Imagine you have already written to a member reminding him that his subscription is overdue. He has ignored this letter. Now something slightly more severe, but still courteous, is required. Write such a letter.

3. Write a letter to a local dignitary suggesting that he might donate a trophy.

30

ASKING A FAVOUR

One of the real tests of a letterwriter's skill is asking a favour. It is the one letter that stands a very good chance of not being particularly welcome.

The approach will depend on the magnitude of the favour and the person from whom it is being asked.

A simple request to an old friend presents no great problem. It can be written in a straightforward, natural style like the one below.

Dear Anne,

I am writing to ask you a favour.

My neighbour's daughter has moved to your district to take up a new job. Unfortunately she has fallen ill and has had to go to hospital.

Since the family live so far away they find it difficult to visit her except at weekends, and she is very lonely. I have promised them that I would write to you and ask if you could look in on her occasionally.

She is in Ward 4, St Mary's. Weekday visiting is from 6 to 7 p.m., and her name is Mary Andrews.

If you could manage to visit her occasionally, she and her family would be extremely grateful, and I would be even more in your debt than I am now.

Yours affectionately,
Joan.

With someone you don't know even a modest request requires a little more formality and a little more persuasion.

Dear Colonel Travers,

After much hesitation I am taking the liberty of writing to ask if you would grant me permission to exercise my dog on your property, Grieve Hill, which slopes right down to my back door.

The previous owner, Mr Browne, used to grant me this concession, and since his death I have had to cross the motorway to Shooter Hollow, which is the only other area where a large dog can obtain sufficient exercise.

My dog is an Alsatian, very docile and well-trained, and I can promise, if permission is granted, that it will cause neither damage nor inconvenience of any kind.

I trust you will give this matter your sympathetic consideration.

Yours faithfully,
Henry Johnstone.

The most difficult favour of all, of course, is asking for a loan.

The writer has to tread a very careful tightrope between sounding persuasive and appearing grovelling. It is a distasteful letter, and the best idea is to face up to it right from the beginning.

A typical borrowing letter might look like this:

Dear Allan,

I greatly regret having to write this letter.

During the past few months I have had a serious run of bad luck. The result is that debts have mounted up, and now total approximately £100.

The position is only temporary. At the end of the year an endowment matures, and I shall be in funds again, but at the moment I find myself in the embarrassing position of being unable to pay my debts.

I wonder if you could possibly lend me the £100? Should you agree I promise I shall repay it the moment I receive my endowment.

Yours sincerely,
Tom.

Exercises

Choose any one of the following:

1. Your brother has just lost his job owing to his firm closing down. Send a letter to a friend of the family, asking him if he could secure a position for your brother in his firm.

2. Your nephew is going on holiday abroad to stay with a pen pal. His mother feels that at thirteen he is too young to be travelling on his own. By chance you have a friend travelling on the same flight. Write to him requesting that he look after the boy.

3. You have opened a small, part-time business. You require a certain machine to make it a success. Your bank manager and all your relatives have already turned you down, but you have a friend who could well afford to lend you the money. Write a letter, putting the suggestion to him.

4. Your neighbour is moving to a new town. You already have a friend in that town. Write suggesting that she might pay a call on the newcomer and generally ensure that she isn't lonely.

31

ABBREVIATIONS AND TECHNICAL TERMS

Every business develops its own shorthand and its own jargon, and the business of letter writing is no exception.

Many of them are relics from a previous age, and although the modern tendency is to use them less and less, they are still to be found, and at least a nodding acquaintance with them is necessary.

Below is a list of the most often used abbreviations and technical terms:

a/c	Account
b & b	Bed and breakfast
carr. pd.	Carriage paid
c/o	Care of (in addresses)
C.O.D.	Cash on delivery
C.W.O.	Cash with order
E. & O.E.	Errors and omissions excepted. (Used in quotations, etc. as a let-out clause for any error which may have crept into the calculations)
e.g.	For example.
et seq.	And following.
ex.	Extra (in advertisements)
F.B.	Full board.
h. & c.	Hot and cold.
i.e.	That is.
Inc.	Incorporated (American for Ltd.)
inst.	This month
inter alia	Among other things.
Ltd.	Limited (after names of firms)
O.H.M.S.	On Her Majesty's Service.
p.p. (per pro)	On behalf of (used when one person is signing on behalf of another)

p. & p.	Postage and packing.
per	Each
pro	For (also used when one person is signing on behalf of another).
prox	Next month.
P.S.	Written afterwards, a postscript.
P.T.O.	Please turn over.
Q.V.	Which see (used when directing someone to seek information in a book)
Re.	With reference to.
R.S.V.P.	Please reply.
S.A.E.	Stamped, addressed envelope.
Stet.	Let it stand, leave it as it was (used when something has been scored out which you wished to remain in)
ult.	Last month.
via	By way of (sometimes used in addresses).
viz	Namely
w.e.f.	With effect from.

Exercises

Write out the following letters and advertisements in full:

(a) Dear Sir,

Herewith our quotation for 240 Martipaks.

240 @ £2.30 per 10.	=	£55.20
p. & p.	=	£3.15
Total (E. & O.E.)	=	£58.35

Our terms are C.W.O. If order received before 27th inst. delivery will be by 4th prox.

Yours faithfully,
A. Temple
p.p. J. Godwin
(Manager)

(b) Seaview, 1 min. prom., B. & B. £1.25, F.B. £2.15, H. & C., T.V., S.A.E. for reply to Graham, 167 Gray Street, Blackpool.

117

(c) Dear Sir,

Re your query of 27th ult., our latest catalogue (Q.V.) lists the complete range we offer. The relevant section will be found on p. 96 et seq.

W. e. f. 17th October our entire stock will be subject to the new tax surcharge of 5%, i.e. 5p in the £.

Terms are C.W.O. or C.O.D.

Yours faithfully,
J. Brown.

Letter to Write

Compose a letter using as many of the abbreviations and technical terms as possible.

32

BUYING BY POST

In recent years the practice of buying by post has increased spectacularly. Thousands of advertisements appear daily in our magazines and newspapers, and hundreds of thousands of customers avail themselves of the service.

The technique of buying by post is precisely the same as for other business letters—be as concise as is consistent with clarity—but it is precisely this business of clarity which causes most trouble. The number of choices offered is usually so bewildering that it is all too easy to omit some vital piece of information.

Look at the following advertisement:

> New solid leather army boots. Sizes 4 to 12. Black or brown, with or without toecaps. Solid leather soles, with steel tips on heels optional. £2.85 or 2 pairs for £5.00. p.p. 22p ex. C.W.O.

Any reply to this advertisement would have to detail the following choices:

- *(a)* size
- *(b)* colour
- *(c)* with or without toecaps
- *(d)* steel tips or no steel tips
- *(e)* one pair or two pairs

A letter ordering a pair would have to look something like this:

Dear Sir,

With reference to your advertisement in today's "Hollworth Courier" I wish to purchase one pair of brown army boots, size 7, with toecaps and steel tips.

I enclose a postal order for £3.07 to cover purchase, postage and packing.

Yours faithfully,
Robert Hutton.

Now examine the following advertisement:

> Full size bureaux. Storage space for books, magazines, stationery, and private papers. 1 m high, 1 m wide, 30 cm deep, superbly finished in whitewood, ready for assembling and painting for only £3.95 carr. 65 p. Fully assembled only £4.95 carr. 75 p. Polished bureau in teak or walnut effect £5.95 carr. 75 p. Or send S.A.E. for details of easy terms.

Any answer to this advertisement would have to state one of three choices—either an unassembled bureau or an assembled, or an assembled bureau in one of two finishes. He would then have to decide whether he wants to buy it outright or send for details of the easy terms.

The finished letter might look like this:

Dear Sir,

I am interested in purchasing one of your fully assembled bureaux at £4.95. I enclose a stamped, addressed envelope for details of your easy terms.

Yours faithfully,
John Jefferson.

Exercises

Examine the following advertisements, then reply to two of them.

(a) Send no money! One of the most beautiful watches ever. Goldplated. 17 jewels. Shock, dust and damp-proof. Swiss made. Send for easy no deposit credit

120

payment terms or 7 days approval at cash price of £7.75. Ladies' model—exactly same price and terms.

(b) Slimline slacks. Extra smart bri-nylon. Hardwearing, strong, wrinkle-free. Ladies' waists: 60 cm–70 cm £1.50, 75 cm–85 cm £2.00, 90 cm–100 cm £2.50, 105 cm–110 cm £3.00. Colours: black, brown, red, navy, green. State second choice. C.W.O. Refund guaranteed.

(c) Gym set, easily assembled, strong rustproof 5 cm tubing, £3 deposit + £1.25 p.p. and 10 instalments at £1.03. Cash £12.25 + £1.25 p.p. C.O.D. 25 p ex. S.A.E. for coloured brochure if preferred.

(d) Popular trellis design candlewick spreads. Diamond tufted with shaped and fringed edges. Assortment of colours includes pink, blue, white, and green. Double size £2.75. Single size—£2.50 p. p. 20 p.

33

MORE AMBITIOUS PERSONAL LETTER— EMOTIONAL

The British are notoriously a stiff upper lip people. They prefer to keep their emotions firmly buttoned up.

There are, however, certain occasions when an emotional letter has to be written. Thoughts that you have never uttered before have to be put down on paper.

During the last war, for instance, before they took off, pilots in the Royal Air Force always wrote a letter to their loved ones, which was to be sent only if they failed to return from the mission.

There are many letters, from all periods of history, which were written in the condemned cell. Here is an extract from a letter written by Anne Boleyn to her husband Henry VIII while awaiting her execution. The dignity of the writing can hardly conceal the strong emotion which underlays this tragic episode in history.

My last and only request shall be, that myself may only bear the burden of your Grace's displeasure, and that it may not touch the innocent souls of those poor gentlemen who, as I understand, are likewise in strait imprisonment for my sake. If ever I have found favour in your sight, if ever the name of Anne Boleyn hath been pleasing in your ears, then let me obtain this request; and I will so leave to trouble your Grace any further; with mine earnest prayers to the Trinity, to have your Grace in his good keeping, and to direct you in all your actions. From my doleful prison in the Tower, this 6th of May. Your most loyal and ever faithful wife,

Anne Boleyn

On a less dramatic scale there is the young woman about to be married, realising suddenly that this is the last night she will spend in her parents' home, and sitting down to write them a letter thanking them for her happy childhood.

The commonest emotional letter is, of course, the love letter.

What a love letter is may be hard to define, but what it most definitely is not is what usually passes for a love letter—a string of trite observations about the weather, etc., interlarded with "darlings", "dearests" and "sweethearts".

Below is a love letter from the past, written by Thomas Carlyle, the famous author, to his future wife on the eve of their marriage:

O my own Jane! I could say so much; but what are words to the sea of thoughts that rolls through my heart when I feel that thou art mine, that I am thine, that henceforth we live not for ourselves but for each other! Let us pray to God that our holy purposes be not frustrated; let us trust in Him and in each other, and fear no evil that can befall us. My last blessing as a lover is with you; this is my last letter to Jane Welsh: my first blessing as a husband, my first kiss to Jane Carlyle is at hand! O my darling, I will always love thee. Good night, then, for the last time we have to part.

I am forever yours,
T. Carlyle.

As a love letter it is appropriately passionate, but to our modern eyes it seems strange after all that passion that the prospective bridegroom should sign himself coldly as "T. Carlyle".

Just as full of emotion as the love letter is its opposite—the letter which puts an end to a love affair, sometimes referred to as a "Dear John" letter. There the dominant emotion is regret, and a typical "Dear John" letter would look like this:

Dear John,

This is the most difficult letter I have ever written in my life.

For months now we have been quarrelling more and more, not merely about trivial things, but about really serious issues. I feel it augurs badly for the future, and the most sensible thing we can do is to admit that we both made a mistake, and end it all while there is still time.

I enclose your ring, very conscious of what it once meant to both of us and how many dreams we built on it.

Try not to think too badly of me. I wish you all the happiness in the world.

Yours regretfully,
Helen.

Exercises

Attempt one of the following:

1. Imagine you are one of the people mentioned in this chapter—an R.A.F. pilot setting off on a mission or a condemned prisoner or a young person leaving home for the first time—and write what you would consider to be a suitable letter for the occasion.

2. Pretend you are the John in the "Dear John" letter and write a suitable letter in reply.

34

THE TELEGRAM

The most concise form of letter writing is the telegram.

Its great advantage is the speed with which it is delivered, but that speed of delivery is expensive. The charge is 25 p. for twelve words or less and 2 p. for every extra word. The words and numbers in the name and address as well as those in the message are counted for charging purposes. So too are the punctuation marks. All of which explains why the style must be so concise.

Let us consider an actual message.

You had intended to spend Saturday with a friend. He had to meet you at 1 p.m. at his local station, but at the very last minute on Friday the boss has told you that he wishes you to go on a business trip the following morning. With promotion prospects in view you can't refuse. Your friend has no telephone, and the only way to get in touch with him in time is by telegram.

You go to the post office and ask for a telegram blank (illustrated below) then set about composing your message.

Charges to pay	POST OFFICE	No.
£	**TELEGRAM**	OFFICE STAMP
RECEIVED	Prefix. Time handed in. Office of Origin and Service Instructions. Words	

From	At ....m
By	To
	By

TO Mʳ JOHN GRAHAM,"LYNDHAM," 9, BARHAM DRIVE,
POLFLEET, BY MARSHAM, KENT.

DEAR JOHN, I AM AFRAID I CAN'T KEEP OUR APPOINTMENT
FOR ONE O'CLOCK AT THE STATION ON SATURDAY. THE BOSS
IS SENDING ME ON A BUSINESS TRIP TO LONDON, AND, WITH
THE ASSISTANT SALES MANAGER'S JOB IN THE OFFING,
I JUST CAN'T REFUSE. I HOPE YOU UNDERSTAND.

YOURS SINCERELY,

BILL

FINAL
DECIMAL

For free repetition of doubtful words telephone "TELEGRAMS ENQUIRY" or call, with this form, B or C at office of delivery. Other enquiries should be accompanied by this form and, if possible, the envelope

B. & S. Ltd. 56-4813 1/71

As a message it is perfectly adequate. It cancels the now obsolete arrangements. It outlines the reason for cancellation. It has, in fact, only one fault—it would cost almost £1.50 to send.

Let us examine it to see how it could be cut down, still retaining everything that is essential.

Take the address first.

Right away one can see the "Mr" is superfluous. With a name like John you are hardly likely to be a Miss or a Mrs.

There is no need either for both the name of the house and its number in the street, and by simply eliminating the house-name, the inverted commas, and the comma before and after it, you save yourself 8 p.

For the same reason one might be tempted to drop the "By Marsham", but that isn't necessary. To prevent customers sending inadequately addressed telegrams the Post Office counts everything in the address after the name of the street as only one word.

The address would therefore appear as:

JOHN GRAHAM
9 BARHAM DRIVE
POLFLEET, BY MARSHAM, KENT.

This counts as only six words, which is in itself a considerable saving, but the real economies are still to be made—on the actual message.

Remember that a telegram should only be used to send urgent messages, then ask yourself what the real urgency is.

It is to stop John turning up at the station at one o'clock on Saturday expecting to spend the whole day with his friend. Anything else—including the reason for the change in the arrangements—has no such urgency. It could all be explained, at greater length and with much greater courtesy, in a letter.

The telegram would then read as follows:

JOHN GRAHAM
9 BARHAM DRIVE
POLFLEET, BY MARSHAM, KENT

CAN'T COME SATURDAY. LETTER FOLLOWS

BILL

Although doing exactly the same job as the first telegram, the second one represents a saving of more than £1.

The economy business, of course, can be carried too far.

There is the famous story of the Aberdonian who, on being told he was to be charged for twelve words anyway, sent the immortal telegram:

"Donaldson, Leverhome Hotel, Ravenswood Road, London. Father died Aberdeen 2 Dundee 1"

There is also the temptation to make up words, e.g. cantcome or willwrite, but all in vain. The Post Office charges all such words as two words.

These are, of course, extreme cases, but over-economy can cause trouble. Take the following case:

FATHER DIED. LETTER FOLLOWS. JOHN.

This leaves out a great deal of urgent information.

When did he die? When is the funeral? Should the recipient come to it? It is useless waiting for a letter. By that time the funeral will be over.

A much better telegram would have been:

FATHER DIED. FUNERAL TUESDAY. PLEASE COME. JOHN.

Telegrams are not always associated with sad occasions. There are many events, such as weddings, which call for a greetings telegram.

Usually these contain some simple message like:

127

CONGRATULATIONS AND BEST WISHES. JOE.

There is also a school of thought, however, that maintains that the best wedding telegram is a funny one, and this leads to such messages as

THREEPENNY PIE WILL NOW COST SIXPENCE. BILL.

Telegrams to Write
Attempt any two of the following:

 (a) Friends are expecting you by train on Friday. You won't be able to arrive until the following Wednesday. Send a telegram to prevent them turning up at the station to meet you.
 (b) On the last day of your holiday you have a car accident, but are not severely injured. They are, however, keeping you under observation for a few hours in hospital, which means that you won't arrive home when you said you would. Send a telegram explaining the situation.
 (c) You have just read that a couple you know have had a baby. Send either a telegram of congratulations or a funny telegram.
 (d) On holiday you have run short of money. Send a telegram home requesting that they send some on to you urgently.
 (e) Send a telegram informing a member of your family of the death of an elderly aunt, but suggest, because of travel difficulties, that he need not attend the funeral.

35

AWKWARD SITUATIONS IN BUSINESS

One situation in business which demands special care is the occasion when things fail to run smoothly.

Complaints may be received about the quality of your goods.

There may be criticisms about late deliveries.

You yourself may have to reprimand one of your own suppliers.

It is now, more than at any other time, that courtesy should be the watchword. If an apology is called for, then, the three rules given for personal apologies in Chapter 20—*Conciliation, Explanation, Reparation*—still hold good.

Let us imagine that a shopkeeper has complained that the last batch of goods you sent contained many which were sub-standard.

A suitable reply might read as follows:

Dear Sir,

We regret to learn that our last consignment of men's cardigans failed to measure up to our usual standards.

We have, of course, a very careful checking process, but it is possible that one batch somehow slipped through unchecked. Our representative will call on you on Tuesday morning, and, if the facts are as stated, rest assured that all faulty garments will be replaced immediately.

Apologising once again for any inconvenience we may have caused, and assuring you of our best services at all times,

I remain,

Yours faithfully,

H. Henderson.

It should be noticed that despite all the courtesy, no uncondi-
tional promises have been made. Put another way the letter might
read:

Dear Sir,

We are not stupid enough to accept your unsupported word
about the quality of our goods.

A representative will call to examine the so-called "faulty"
garments and if—and only if—HE decides they are sub-standard,
shall we consent to replace them.

Yours faithfully,
H. Henderson.

It will be readily seen, however, which is the better business
letter.

Even when you are the injured party the same courteous
approach should be maintained. Anger all too often breeds
anger. It may well be that a genuine mistake has been made and
that your supplier will be only too anxious to put it right, and, in
the first instance at least, it is always wise to give him
that opportunity.

Dear Sir,

I regret to inform you that your last consignment of cigarette
lighters has been causing considerable trouble. This week alone
customers have returned four of them, which were not function-
ing properly.

Knowing the high reputation of your products I am losing no
time in bringing this matter to your attention, and confidently
await your reply.

Yours faithfully,
Alan Short.

There must be, of course, times when a complaint is completely unjustified and absolutely no promises of reparation are possible. The only course then is to state the facts as politely as possible.

Dear Sir,

We regret that some of the ball-point pens you bought from us are being returned by customers.

We should point out, however, that our representative made it quite clear that, at the prices we were quoting, the pens came from rejected export stock, and that many were sub-standard.

Yours faithfully,
Henry Clive.

No situation in business demands so much care as demanding money.

Ideally every client should pay his bill within days of receiving it. Unfortunately this does not always happen. Many clients are dilatory in this respect, and the letter writer is then left with the problem of asking for his money and yet avoiding giving offence to the customer.

The initial request presents no difficulties. The bill, with some such covering letter as the following, is all that is required.

Dear Sir,

Please find enclosed our bill for £14.50.

Yours faithfully,
J. Dunn.

If this is ignored, the writer can still afford to be perfectly courteous.

Dear Sir,

We discover that the account sent to you on 14th April has not yet been paid.

We realise that this is obviously an oversight, and should be pleased if you could rectify it at your earliest convenience.

Yours faithfully,
J. Dunn.

It is when this letter is ignored that the real difficulty begins.

The non-payment is now obviously more than an oversight, and it is useless to go on pretending that it is. A new approach is required, and there are several choices.

There is the sympathetic approach:

Dear Sir,

We regret to have to send you our account for the third time.

If there is any reason why you cannot pay in full at the moment, then a letter outlining these reasons would enable us to consider what arrangements can be made.

Yours faithfully,
J. Dunn.

There is the appeal to logic:

Dear Sir,

This is the third time we have sent out our account.

We have our own financial obligations to meet and must insist that you meet yours.

Yours faithfully,
J. Dunn.

There is the curt approach:

Dear Sir,

This is the third time we have rendered our account.
Kindly remit by return.

Yours faithfully,
J. Dunn.

Finally there is the threatening approach:

Dear Sir,

Your account is now nine months overdue.

If you do not pay by return you leave us no choice but to take legal action.

Yours faithfully,
J. Dunn.

Exercises

Attempt one of the following:

1. Compose a letter from a shopkeeper complaining of faulty goods, then compose a reply from the manufacturer, dealing with the complaint.

2. You have a customer to whom you have sent an account for £25.75. He has not yet paid it. Send him three increasingly severe letters at 6 weekly intervals, demanding payment.

36

LETTER WRITING AND CITIZENSHIP

In Chapter 23 (Letters To The Editor) you will have noticed that many of the topics touched on were topics which turn up again and again in such subjects as Civics or Liberal Studies.

This is perhaps the most important function of the letter to the editor. It gives the ordinary citizen the chance to air his views on controversial subjects and offers him the opportunity of helping to sway public opinion.

Every great issue of our times has been debated and fought out in the correspondence columns of our national and local press.

Nowhere else is democracy seen so clearly at work. Nowhere else is it quite so obvious that in politics there is no such thing as a straightforward issue. For every person who honestly supports one view there is another one who holds just as sincerely the diametrically opposite opinion, and, even more important, they are all ready to back their opinions with good solid arguments.

Below is a selection of the controversial issues of our times and the type of correspondence it has provoked in our newpapers.

A. *Crime And Punishment*

Dear Sir,

How courageous of our M.P.'s to abolish the death penalty. It was time this barbaric law was off our statute books.

Each time I learned that someone was to be legally murdered in our name I found the burden of my tiny share of the guilt unbearable. No one but God has the right to take a life.

Yours etc.,

Dear Sir,

Your correspondent's tender conscience does her credit, but as a policeman's wife I cannot share her admiration of our M.P.'s for abolishing the death penalty.

The death penalty was a powerful deterrent. What happens if my husband now tries to arrest a bank robber? If captured the thief will already get 15 years, so it is only logical that he will shoot his way out of trouble. He will get no stiffer sentence if he happens to murder my husband in the process.

Yours, etc.,

Dear Sir,

While sympathising with the policeman's wife I feel she is allowing personal feelings to cloud the issue. Statistics prove that the death penalty was no real deterrent. A life sentence is just as harsh a punishment, but it has the tremendous advantage of being less final, and if new evidence comes to light later, then the mistake can be rectified.

Make a mistake with the death penalty and it is made for ever.

I think that all those who advocate the death penalty should be forced to witness a hanging, just to see what a horrible affair it is.

Yours etc.,

Dear Sir,

Your correspondent this week seems very sure that the death penalty was no deterrent, and suggests that a life sentence is just as harsh a punishment. If this is so, can he say why every convicted murderer in the past immediately put in a plea to have the death sentence commuted to one of life imprisonment?

He also suggests that people like myself should be forced to witness a hanging. I suggest that if he wants to test his views properly he should not do it in the comfort of these columns. He should try them out on the widow of one of the victims of these thugs.

Yours etc.,

135

B. *The National Health Service*

The N.H.S. was introduced to Britain just after the war. In return for a weekly payment by the wage-earner everyone in his family is entitled to free medical treatment and to dental and optical treatment at vastly reduced rates.

Dear Sir,

The National Health Service has killed forever the old close relationship between the family doctor and his patient.

We are now merely numbers, part of the grey uniformity that is modern Britain. The doctor has no interest in his patients. He gets his money anyway, whether you are healthy or ill.

His surgery is full of people with minor illnesses, who could quite easily cure themselves with a couple of aspirins, but who have been bitten by the something-for-nothing welfare bug. These are the people he is forced to spend his energies on, leaving little time for the genuinely ill.

It is a fiasco, pure and simple, and the sooner we get back to the old system the better it will be for the practice of medicine in this country.

Yours, etc.,

Dear Sir,

I have just returned from a country where they practise the old system of medicine, the U.S.A. All that means is that the doctors feel your wallet before they feel your pulse!

When I left, the newspapers were carrying the story of a man who stumbled into a hospital carrying his injured child. His financial status was checked at the desk, he was refused admission and directed to the so-called "free" hospital several miles away. By the time he got there his child was dead.

That may be the way medicine should be practised, but if it is, then I have only one thing to say.

Thank heavens for the "grey uniformity" of modern Britain.

Yours, etc.,

C. *The Common Market*

The Common Market is a group of Western European countries. Inside their borders they allow free trade and free movement of population among members. No issue in recent years has caused more controversy than Britain's decision to apply for membership.

Dear Sir,

The Common Market is the greatest opportunity ever offered to Britain.

If we refuse to join we shall be cut off from Western Europe, unable to sell any of our products there.

As we all know, we can only grow enough food to feed about half our population.

With us it's a case of export or die, and if we fail to grasp our opportunity now, then, unlike some, I wouldn't say we'll turn into a second class nation. I say we'll turn into a third class nation —a small, unimportant offshore island of Europe.

Yours, etc.,

Dear Sir,

I'm glad your correspondent is so sure about the Common Market. I only wish I could share his confidence.

As far as I can understand from our M.P.'s our food is going to cost us a lot more when we join. If we can stave off starvation long enough, however, they assure us our wages will rise to the same standard of those in Common Market countries, and we shall all finish up better off.

This is very reassuring, but only this week a shipyard owner was over here from Dunkirk, attracted by unemployment in British shipyards. He hoped to recruit several hundred workmen for his shipyard, but discovered to his chagrin that nobody wanted to come. The wages he was offering were only about 75% of the normal rate for a shipyard worker in Britain.

Which rather knocks on the head the cosy theories about the higher wages in the Common Market.

Yours, etc.,

Exercises

Write two letters—one for and one against—on any one of the following subjects:

1. Raising the school leaving age to 16.
2. Arming our police.
3. The case for—and against—fee paying schools.
4. Votes at 16.
5. Long hair for men.
6. Should our doctors be allowed to strike?
7. The House of Lords—a good thing or a bad thing?
8. Should old age pensions be raised? Remember that the money will have to come from increased taxes.

37

CONFIRMING A PHONE CALL

In many ways today the telephone has taken over the role of the letter, especially in the business world.

It has many advantages. It is speedy and efficient, and questions can be posed and answered in a matter of seconds that would take several days if left to the usual processes of business correspondence.

It has, however, one serious disadvantage. No record is left of the transaction. There is nothing that can be filed. There is no proof of what actually took place beyond the evidence of the two people who took part in the telephone conversation.

Let a prospective client 'phone and book rooms for a fortnight in a hotel, for example, then fail to turn up. The manager, who has no doubt turned other clients away, is now left with the vacant rooms. He has undoubtedly a legal case for compensation, but he has no proof. The client can, if he likes, claim that he made no phone call.

It has therefore become the custom when booking accommodation by telephone to confirm it almost immediately by letter.

A confirmatory letter to a hotel would look like this:

Dear Sir,

Further to our telephone conversation of yesterday I confirm that I wish to book two double rooms at your hotel from 27th August to 14th September.

Yours faithfully,
John Mansfield.

Occasionally a deposit is asked for and the letter would then read like this:

Dear Sir,

Further to our telephone conversation today I am writing to confirm my booking of a single room at your hotel from June 14th to June 28th.

I enclose a cheque for £5 as a deposit.

Yours faithfully,
Edward Lendall.

Exercises

Attempt any one of the following:

1. By telephone you have reserved a single room for a week in a small boarding house. Confirm it by letter.

2. You have just placed an order by phone for 100 1 cm planks, 2 m 60 cm long by 20 cm inches wide. The supplier has asked you to confirm the order by letter. Do so now.

3. You have just cancelled by telephone your booking of two single rooms for a fortnight in a seaside hotel. Confirm the cancellation by letter.

38

LETTER OF REFERENCE

In the chapters dealing with the application for a job the two methods of gauging the character of an applicant were outlined.

One was to demand letters of reference, and the other was to ask for the names of referees whom the firm could then contact and question about the applicant's character.

There comes a stage in the career of most of us when we are called upon to write such a reference. The points to be listed are straightforward enough—how long you have known the candidate, in what capacity, and how his character and abilities have impressed you during that period.

If the reference is to be a glowing one there is no difficulty whatsoever. A letter like the following will suffice:

Dear Sir,

It is a pleasure to recommend a man of John Graham's calibre.

Coming to our firm in October, 1967 as a junior clerk, he remained with us until June, 1970, when he left to better his position.

During that time he proved himself to be a conscientious, courteous and extremely able member of my staff. He was popular with colleagues and customers alike, and could always be relied upon to give of his best, whether supervised or un-supervised.

I recommend him without reservation for any clerical post of responsibility.

> Yours faithfully,
> Keith Burroughs
> (Accounts Manager)

It is when the reference is intended to be not quite so enthusiastic that the difficulties occur. Take the extreme case of an employee who was unsatisfactory in every way. When it comes to writing a reference for him you might be tempted to take your revenge in the following manner:

Dear Sir,
John Harris was the laziest, scruffiest, most incompetent employee it was ever my misfortune to meet. If you are thinking of giving him a berth, make it a wide one!

Yours truthfully,
Alan Smith
(Manager)

Apart altogether from the fairness of the matter, this would be a most unwise reference to write. It is actionable, and in a court of law you might have to justify your highly intemperate language and colourful charges.

By far the most effective way with such references is to write the barest minimum that is required of you:

Dear Sir,
John Harris was employed as a storeman with our firm from 14th November, 1968. He left on 12th September, 1969.

Yours faithfully,
Alan Smith
(Manager)

To any prospective employer the complete lack of enthusiasm is evident.

When your name has been given as a referee you are on firmer ground. Then the prospective employer will write you a letter, asking for specific information.

142

Dear Sir,

Mr John Harris, who has applied for a position with us, has given your name as a referee.

I wonder if you could oblige us with your own estimate of his character and abilities.

A stamped, addressed envelope is enclosed for your reply.

> Yours faithfully,
> James Edgar
> (Personnel Officer)

Having been asked specifically by a prospective employer for your professional opinion, you are now in a privileged position. You can now safely commit to paper your honest opinion, and might reply as follows:

Dear Sir,

With reference to your enquiry of 14th May, John Harris was employed by us as a storeman from 14th November, 1968 to 12th September, 1969. I regret to say that his work proved unsatisfactory, and we eventually dismissed him.

> Yours faithfully,
> Alan Smith
> (Manager)

Exercises

Write one of the following letters:

1. You are a shop manager. Write a glowing reference for a former shop assistant who is now applying for the post of manager with another firm.

2. A former employee has asked you for a reference. She was a cheerful, popular person, but inclined to be careless. Write a reference for her which brings out these points.

3. A firm has written to you about a prospective employee who has given your name. One of the essential qualities demanded by them is punctuality. While he was with you their prospective employee was frequently in trouble for lateness and absenteeism. Reply suitably.

4. An ex-employee, who has given your name as a referee, was, while in your employment, suspected of pilfering and eventually dismissed. No legal action was taken. Reply to his prospective employer's letter of enquiry.

39

LETTERS FROM THE PAST

In Chapter 28 we discussed the business methods of a previous age.

In this chapter we are going to examine a few personal letters from the past. They come from an age when manners were more formal and language more flowery than in our own times. The greetings and the endings are much more stylised, and their whole construction completely lacks the freer, more friendly atmosphere of today.

The first is from a soldier son to his father:

Honoured Sir,

Your letter is now come to hand by the latest carrier requesting my intelligences. I hasten to reply and to thank you for your most gracious offer, which I must decline for at present I have no need of your services, being in cash again.

Ireland, I fear, is but a sorry posting for a soldier. The country-side is desolate in the extreme and wanting in those refinements pleasing to polite society.

My lodging is hard by a village which has little to offer but one mean hostelry, dirty beyond description. This pleasure is little to my taste, hence for exercise I will ride and shoot, and for my entertainment I shall cultivate my reading, from which I hope to gain some profit.

My solitary consolation in my troubled state is that the turn of service comes round and three years will pass.

Commend me to my mother and my sisters and inform them that I am longing to be in their society once more. Till then I have the honour to be, Sir, your obedient and affectionate son,

Jonathan Hardacre.

The second letter is written by Andrew Marvell, who was a very famous poet. He had performed some minor service for the Wardens of Trinity House. This is his thank-you letter for a gift they sent him in return for his services:

Gentlemen, my worthy friends,

I found myself very much surprised lately by a Token which you were pleased to send me by Mr Coates. And truly I was very unwilling to have accepted, having always desired rather to do those offices of friendship where I could have no prospect of other gratification than the goodness of the action. But you especially ought not to have placed any such reward upon me, whom you have continually engaged by all manner of civil obligations. Nevertheless your Warden used so pressing an importunity with me (if courtesy may be so styled) that I could not decline it. Therefore I do by the same hand return you my thanks desiring that you will find out some further way that I may work out what I have not deserved of you otherwise than by my good affection always toward you and your worthy Society. So, wishing you all happiness, I remain,

      Gentlemen etc:

        Your very affectionate friend to serve you.

         Andrew Marvell.

The third is a newspaper correspondence which appeared in the Public Advertiser during the second half of the eighteenth century on the subject of Lord Granby, the commander-in-chief of the army.

146

Letter 1

Sir,

It has lately been a fashion to pay a compliment to the bravery and generosity of the commander-in-chief at the expense of his understanding.

They who love him least make no question of his courage. Admitting him to be as brave as a total absence of all feeling and reflection can make him, let us see what sort of merit he derives from the remainder of his character. If it be a generosity to accumulate in his own person and family a number of lucrative employments and to heap promotions upon his favourites and dependants, the commander-in-chief is the most generous man alive.

This, sir, is the detail.

And if the discipline of the army be in any degree preserved, what thanks are due to a man whose cares, notoriously confined to filling up vacancies, have degraded the office of commander-in-chief into a broker of commissions?

Junius.

Letter 2

Sir,

The Kingdom swarms with such numbers of felonious robbers of private character and virtue, that no honest or good man is safe; especially as these cowardly base assassins stab in the dark, without having the courage to sign their real names to their malevolent and wicked productions. No man who knows Lord Granby can possibly hear so good and great a character most vilely abused, without a warm and just indignation against this Junius.

A very long, uninterrupted, impartial friendship with Lord Granby gives me the right to affirm that all Junius' assertions are false and scandalous. Lord Granby's courage, though of the brightest and most ardent kind, is among the lowest of his numerous good qualities. A sincere love and attachment to his king and country impelled him to the field, where he never gained aught but honour. Can a man who is described as "unfeeling and void of reflection" be constantly employed in seeking proper objects on whom to exercise those glorious virtues of compassion and generosity?

He is next attacked for being unfaithful to his promises and engagements. Where are Junius' proofs? Though I could give some instances where a breach of promise would be a virtue, especially in the case of those who would pervert the open unsuspecting moments of convivial mirth into sly applications for preferment, and would endeavour to surprise a good man, who cannot bear to see anyone leave him dissatisfied, into unguarded promises.

William Draper.

Some letters from the past reveal the character and wit of eminent persons in a particular way. Consider for example this letter from a famous writer Sir Herbert Beerbohm Tree, in reply to a request to read a manuscript by a would-be dramatist.

My Dear Sir,
    I have read your play.

Oh, my dear Sir,
Yours faithfully,

Not all the letters from the past are good, well-written letters. Naturally the bad ones haven't been preserved, except in the literature of the period, where they were written for their comic effect.

The examples below are from "Pickwick Papers" by Charles Dickens.

The first is a letter to Sam Weller from Tony Weller.

My dear Sammle,

I am wery sorry to have the pleasure of bein the Bear of ill news your mother-in-law cort cold consekens of imprudently setting too long on the damp grass in the rain the doctor says that if she'd swallo'd varm brandy & vater artervards insted of afore she mightn't have been no vus your Father had hopes as she vould have vorked round as usual but just as she wos a turnen the corner my boy she took the wrong road and vent down hill with a welocity you never see for she paid the last pike at twenty minutes afore six o'clock yesterday evenin by the vay your Father says that if you will come and see me Sammy he vill take it as a wery great Favor for I am wery lonely Samivel and am Samivel infernally yours —

Tony Weller

The second is a love letter written by Sam Weller as a Valentine:

Lovely creetur,

I feel myself ashamed, and completely circumscribed in a dressin' of you, for you are a nice gal and nothin' but it.

Afore I see you, I thought all women was alike. But now I find what a reglar soft-headed, ink-red'lous turnip I must ha' been; for there ain't nobody like you, though I like you better than nothin' at all.

So I take the privilege of the day, Mary, my dear, to tell you that the first and only time I see you, your likeness was took on my hart in much quicker time and brighter colours than ever a likeness was took by the profeel macheen (which p'raps you may have heerd on Mary my dear) altho' it does finish a portrait and put the frame and glass on completely with a hook at the end to hang it up by, and all in two minutes and a quarter.

Except of me Mary my dear as your walentine and think over what I've said. My dear Mary I will now conclude.

Your love-sick,
Pickwick.

The "profeel macheen" mentioned in the letter was an early type of camera which produced a silhouette.

Why Sam Weller signs his letter with the name of his friend, requires a little explanation. The best way to do this is quote the relevant passage from the book—a conversation between Sam and his father about the unsigned letter Sam has just written.

"That's rayther a sudden pull-up, ain't it, Sammy?" inquired Mr Weller.

"Not a bit on it", said Sam, "she'll vish there wos more, and that's the great art o' letter-writin'".

"Well," said Mr Weller, "there's somethin' in that; and I wish your mother-in-law 'ud only conduct her conwersation on the same genteel principle. Ain't you a-goin' to sign it?"

"That's the difficulty," said Sam. "I don't know what to sign it".

"Sign it Veller," said the oldest surviving proprietor of that name.

"Won't do," said Sam. "Never sign a walentine with your own name."

"Sign it 'Pickvick' then," said Mr Weller; "it's a wery good name, and a easy one to spell."

"The wery thing," said Sam. "I could end with a werse". Sam was not to be dissuaded from the poetical idea that had occurred to him, so he signed the letter,

"Your love-sick
Pickwick"

150

Exercises

Write the letter from the soldier as a modern son might write it to his father

or

Write for Andrew Marvell a modern letter of thanks to the Wardens of Trinity House

or

Rewrite the newspaper correspondence as it might appear in a modern newspaper.

or

Write one of the letters from "Pickwick Papers" as a modern, educated person might write it.

40

THE SET SITUATION—THE LOCAL NEWSPAPER

Of all the situations which give practice in letter writing, none is quite so productive as the local newspaper.

Within its pages lies the raw material for most of the letter types which have been taught in this book.

Below, divided into sections, will be found a representative selection of the kind of items likely to be found in it.

Section 1

ANNOUNCEMENTS

Births

ROBINSON—At the Largie Memorial Hospital on 3rd August, 1971 to **ROBERT** and **JEAN** (Wilson), 10 Park Avenue, Carlton, a daughter (Suzanne); both well.

CONNOR—At the Royal Maternity Hospital on 4th August, 1971 to **CATHERINE** (Campbell), wife of Dr Samuel Frame, Pineview, Hallend Road, Carlton, a daughter, both well.

Engagements

FORMBY—GALSTON

The engagement is announced between **MURIEL**, youngest daughter of Mr and Mrs J. Galston, 64 Hallworth Crescent, Hallworth and **EDWARD**, elder son of Mr and Mrs K. Formby, 2 Riverside Road, Carlton.

Marriages

WATSON—DUDLEY—At St Mary's Church, Hallworth, on 4th August, 1971, by the Rev. D. H. Collins, **ALBERT**, only son of Mrs A. Watson and the late Mr Andrew Watson, 12 Westview Avenue, Carlton, to JEAN, youngest daughter of Mr and Mrs L. Dudley, 40, Blockville Road, Hallworth.

Deaths

RUSSELL—At Largie Memorial Hospital, on 4th August, 1971, ISABELLA JONES, dearly loved wife of John Russell, 22 Blockville Road, Hallworth.
OWENS—Suddenly at his home, Tafts Farm, Carlton, on 6th August, 1971, RICHARD OWENS, beloved husband of Alice Kemp.

Section 2

EMPLOYMENT

AGENTS, men or women, required in all areas, selling ingenious household gadget. Mechanical aptitude and current driving licence essential. Smith, 14 High Street, Carlton.
CLERK/CLERKESS. Age 18 to 20 years. Commencing salary £564 per annum, rising by annual increments to £965. Apply in writing giving details of age, education, etc. to the Secretary, Glendale Hospital, Glendale, Lancs.

Section 3

FOR SALE

School blazers from £2.50! Blazers—navy-blue, brown, green—to fit 5–7 years £2.50; 8–11 years £3; 12–15 years £3.50; 16–18 years £4. With badges 70p extra. All local badges in stock. Send chest size, height and age and name of school. C.W.O. Refund guaranteed. The Blazer Specialist, High Street, Carlton.
Modern Fireplaces from £15 each. Tiled. Easy clean hearth. Ordinary or Baxi fires. Ask our representative to call or send S.A.E. for coloured brochure. Grant, Market Square, Hallworth.

ARTICLES WANTED

Wanted, pair of Gents Boots, size 7. J. Warwick, 7 Blondel Road, Carlton.

£20 paid for good second hand fridge. Waddell, 8 Springhill Avenue, Lowe-on-Sea.

Section 5

READERS' LETTERS

Dear Sir,

I really must protest at the announcement that the government spent £205 million last year in aid to the developing countries. With our own pensioners going cold in the winter I consider it monstrous. Charity begins at home.

Yours faithfully,
R. Dickinson.

Exercises

Attempt one letter from each section.

In Section 1 write a letter of congratulations or a letter of sympathy to one of the people mentioned in the announcements.

In Section 2 apply for one of the jobs advertised.

In Section 3 purchase one of the items offered for sale.

In Section 4 imagine that you own one of the items and write offering to sell it to the advertiser.

Finally, in Section 5, write a letter to the editor either agreeing or disagreeing with the letter published.

After you Write The Letter

We have now learned how to write a letter. In Chapter 3 we learned about addressing the envelope. What happens after that is also an interesting story.

The first step, of course, is to stick on the stamp. By convention it is stuck on the top right hand corner, although there is no law or regulation which insists it should go there. Later, however, you will learn why it is wiser to obey the convention.

In Britain the letter is placed in a postbox. If you happen to live in another part of the world you will know how your letters are collected; not all countries have the same arrangements but in Britain the postman collects letters from the postbox in a mail van and takes them to the nearest sorting office. In a city this will be situated in the city itself. In the country it might be in the nearest market town.

The first process the letters are subjected to in a large sorting office is "facing". This means they are all made to "face" in the same way with all the stamps in approximately the same place. This is done so that they can be fed into a machine which cancels the stamps.

It is here that the folly of sticking the stamp anywhere but in the top right hand corner will become evident. All letters that cannot be readily "faced" are put aside to be cancelled by hand.

To cancel (or frank) means to mark the stamp in such a way that it cannot be re-used. This is done by means of a postmark which shows the name of the post office and the date of posting.

After cancelling, sorters put the letters into pigeon-holes according to the places to which they are going. The letters for any one place are collected in a mailbag, which is sealed and is sent off by rail or by mail van.

When the mailbag arrives at its destination the letters are sorted by local postmen into streets and are delivered by them on their rounds.

If the letters are going a distance—from Edinburgh to London, for instance—they will be carried in a train called a Travelling Post Office (T.P.O.). All the letters for England will be put on this train. Inside it is fitted out like a sorting office, and sorting is carried on throughout the journey. Mailbags can be picked up en route without the necessity of stopping the train. The mailbags are suspended on special arms at stations on the way and are picked up in nets hung out from the side of the express as it hurtles through. Sorted mailbags can be dropped off in the same way, but this time the special arm is on the express and the net at the wayside station.

If you intend your letter to go abroad the process becomes even more complicated.

Let us say you are writing to California in the U.S.A. What is going to happen to your letter after it leaves Britain? It carries a British stamp, which is your receipt for the fee you paid to the British Post Office. To the US Post Office you have paid absolutely nothing.

When your letter is put ashore at New York why should they go to all the trouble of collecting it, sorting it, transporting it the huge distance to California, then delivering it safely? The same question can be asked if you happen to live in some other part of the world, say Nigeria or Australia. Wherever you live you have purchased a stamp issued in the country of origin but you have paid nothing to the Post Office in the country to which your letter is destined.

The answer is that the country abroad belongs—like almost every other country in the world—to an organisation called Universal Postal Union. Member nations agree to handle the mail of all other member nations free of charge. The US Post will deliver your letter to California, but in return the British Post Office will deliver any reply your Californian friend cares to send you in Britain.

Sending a letter abroad is also complicated by the fact that you have two choices. It can go by sea or it can go by air.

Sea mail has its disadvantages. The chief one is that it is slow. Your letter to California could well take several weeks before it is delivered.

Air mail on the other hand is much faster. Your letter will arrive in any part of the world within days. The real disadvantage of airmail is that it is expensive. The weight of mail that can be carried in a plane is limited. If you wish to send a bulky letter and take up more than your fair share of that weight you will have to pay for it.

If you are sending a letter by airmail it has therefore become the custom to buy specially thin airmail notepaper. Specially thin airmail envelopes are on sale too. They usually have a highly coloured border so that they are easily spotted by sorters, and bear the slogan "Airmail" and its French equivalent "Par Avion." Special airmail letters are also sold which combine the notepaper and envelope in one continuous very thin sheet.

If you are sending a letter to the continent of Europe, however, there are now so many planes on these busy routes that all letters are carried by airmail whether they are marked that way or not.

Even in mail within Britain there are certain other complications which can arise.

If you are sending money or anything valuable by post, for an extra charge your letter can be registered. This provides the sender with proof of posting in the form of a numbered receipt. The postman will also insist on the receiver signing as proof of delivery. If the letter is lost the Post Office will pay compensation.

If you merely wish proof of posting rather than insurance against loss, for a smaller fee you will be issued with a Certificate of Posting.

If, on the other hand, it is speed of delivery you desire, then for another extra fee you can send your letter by Express Post. The letter is sent by normal means until it reaches the post office of its destination. From there it is sent out immediately by special messenger.

Although the sending of letters is now so commonplace it was only in 1840 that the first postage stamp was invented. Before that time postage was an expensive business. The rate depended on the distance travelled and the number of pages in the letter.

Then in 1840 Britain introduced the first stamp, the famous penny black showing the head of Queen Victoria. Its inventor, Rowland Hill, reasoned that it was more profitable to carry a large number of cheap letters than a few expensive ones, and although postal rates have increased many times since then, it is interesting to note that they are still cheaper today than they were before 1840.